NOW THAT SHOT SUCKED!

Golf's Mental Game for Duffers

BILL RILEY

PAGE PUBLISHING
Conneaut Lake, PA

First originally published by Page Publishing 2022

ISBN 979-8-88654-315-5 (pbk)
ISBN 979-8-88654-316-2 (digital)

Printed in the United States of America

To Dad, who taught me the game;
and Randy, who taught me the mental game.

Chapter 1

Introduction

Golf, perhaps more than any other sport, places a premium on mental and emotional performance. Managing yourself on the course is often the difference between enjoying a round and wanting to give away your clubs after a round. Sports psychologists have developed numerous tips and strategies to improve the mental game of golfers. There is no shortage of mental tips and recommendations for golfers to apply to their game. Then why yet another book on golf's mental game? Because these mental game tips are typically applicable to pros and low handicappers, not to the average weekend duffer.

It makes sense that golf's mental game instruction is most applicable to tour pros and scratch golfers. Sports psychology consultants don't make their money or reputations working with high handicappers; they make their money and reputations working with tour pros and competitive amateurs who have money and time to spend on their mental game. They work with highly skilled golfers, not those of us who feel fortunate to make solid contact. They work with golfers who have top-of-the-line, fitted equipment, not decade-old off-the-rack clubs. They work with golfers who spend nearly every day playing golf, not those of us who feel lucky if we can get on the course once every week or two. As a result, mental game instruction seldom has the weekend duffer in mind.

For example, most sports psychologists will encourage you to visualize the shot before you hit it. For low handicappers, this strategy is helpful because they can visualize a shot they have produced many times, and their brain can rehearse the complex series of neuromuscular processes that have produced that shot in the past. For a high handicapper, visualizing a shot often is of little or no benefit because we don't have enough trials hitting the shot we envision. It is like asking most of us to visualize pole vaulting. Since we have no experience pole vaulting well, or at all for that matter, the visual image we produce has no relationship to what our body is supposed to do. Since most of us have never pole vaulted, the only image we can conjure up is from the third-person perspective. We picture pole vaulting from the perspective of the TV camera, not from the perspective of the person doing the vaulting.

The high handicap golfer has the same experience when trying to visualize certain golf shots. You can picture a high draw all you want, but if you've seldom hit that shot, you will probably picture the shot as you have observed it being hit by others, not by you. More importantly, your body can't use this image to produce a swing that results in a high draw because you haven't hit that shot enough for your brain to know intuitively how to reproduce it. Of course, you can probably visualize that low, screaming, banana ball slice, but that isn't going to do much to improve your game.

Another significant difference between the mental game for pros and low handicappers versus mid to high handicappers is the goal of playing. Most mental game tactics are relevant to the tournament context in which the pressures of competition place a premium on performing optimally under pressure. There are often real stakes on the line, and a missed putt can result in thousands in lost prize money or not getting a tour exemption. As a result, most golf psychology books focus on optimizing the performance of each shot and doing so in pressure situations.

For recreational golfers, the goal is mostly to have fun. Yes, we'd like to play well, but there is no real pressure, no real stakes on the line. How we play a round has no impact on our daily lives—we still come home to our families and our regular jobs. And the only financial impact of playing poorly is that we lose a few dollars in friendly bets to keep the round interesting. We don't play golf to win; we play golf to have fun. Of course, playing well is correlated with having fun during the round, but all too often duffers forget that the purpose of the round is to have fun and not let a bad round spoil what otherwise is a nice day outdoors with friends. A golf psychology book for duffers needs to improve performance, but always in the context of playing golf to have fun.

As a psychologist by training and a typical recreational golfer because my day job got in the way of playing golf more often, I have had many opportunities to observe the application and misapplication of these sports psychology principles to the typical duffer. I know duffers. I have played with them regularly over the nearly fifty years that I've played golf. They are my friends, my family, my neighbors, and me. Every duffer at multiple times in every round provides an excellent case study on how not to manage the mental game of golf.

Some would argue that it is a waste of time to improve the mental game of the average recreational golfer. There is some truth to the sentiment that the average golfer needs a teaching pro, not a sports psychologist. No amount of psychological wizardry can cause a bad golfer to be good, and nothing in this book will fix a bad swing. If you can't make solid contact with the ball and send it in the general direction you are aiming, then put down this book, pick up the phone, and set up an appointment for golf lessons. However, if you have a passable swing and can usually make solid contact, then you probably can benefit more, not less, from improving your mental game compared to a scratch golfer.

Golf is a game of transitions—from shot to shot, hole to hole, front nine to back nine, round to round—and these transitions are much more important for the average golfer who far more often has to transition from a horrible shot or horrible hole or horrible round than does a pro or scratch golfer. Each transition is an opportunity to regain your composure and think strategically about the next shot. Compared to pros and low handicappers, duffers have many more opportunities per round to improve their game by managing their mental game during these transitions. You don't have to be a great golfer to benefit from learning how to better manage the course and yourself.

Do you typically end a round saying, "If only I hadn't blown up on (insert hole number here), I would have broken 90 (or 100) today?" If so, then this book is for you. The mental strategies described are tailored to the average recreational golfer. Although hopefully also entertaining, the content is consistent with the latest research in performance psychology but adapted for the game of the recreational golfer. The end of each chapter has "take it to the course" reminders, so you can incorporate this instruction into your game as quickly as possible. Managing your mental game can improve your scores, but more importantly, it can make the game more enjoyable to play.

Chapter 2

Preparation

If you are a recreational golfer, by definition, you probably do little to prepare between rounds for playing golf. You *play* golf; you don't *practice* golf. For most duffers, preparation between rounds consists mostly of watching golf on television. However, there are a number of things you can do between rounds to be better prepared mentally and physically to play good golf.

But wait, I thought this was a book about the mental game; what's up with this chapter about practicing? Well, there are a couple of ways to build confidence: one that works and one that doesn't. The one that doesn't is all the self-affirmation talk. To paraphrase the *Saturday Night Live* character, Stuart Smalley, you may be good enough, and smart enough, and doggone it, people like you, but that won't make you a good golfer. There's a reason why Stuart Smalley is a satirical character. You can tell yourself all you want that you're a good golfer and deserve to shoot a good score, but real confidence comes from experience, not from simply telling yourself that you're good. Confidence on the course comes from having the experience of hitting good shots, even if you're not hitting good shots today. You want to build the confidence to persevere through a bad patch in your game. You may have just shanked a ball into the woods, but you've experienced being able to correct that and hit the ball solid the next time. You may be struggling to control your slice, but you've experienced being able to keep the slice under control. Since most duffers are lucky to get in more than one or two rounds a month, the best place to learn these confidence lessons is on the practice range.

Practice range

Practice may never make perfect, but it does improve how you play. The primary advice is simple: go to the practice range. Most recreational golfers don't play enough rounds to get better, but getting to the practice range on any week you don't play will at least keep your game from deteriorating and keep you prepared to play. Most importantly, it builds confidence in your game based on real experiences, not based on some faux self-affirmation that you haven't earned.

Once you get to the range, there are a number of things you can do to practice better and improve your mental game.

Get the smallest bucket of balls possible. The practice range entices you with the "get three times the balls for twice the price" offer, but you don't need to hit that many golf balls. Your body probably isn't physically fit enough to hit that many balls without muscle fatigue. As you get tired, you get sloppy. How many times have you started out hitting the ball pretty well at the practice range only to get worse near the end? Part of the problem is that you got tired, both physically and mentally. The practice range is not a test of golf endurance. On the practice range, less is better.

How many balls do you usually hit during a round of golf? Even if you usually shoot around 100, you don't hit 100 shots. If we assume that your putting is better than the rest of your game, then you two-putt every green, so that's 36 strokes. Let's also assume that you don't "chilly-dip" any of your chips and have only one chip per hole—that's 18 more shots. That leaves you with 46 shots that are like the ones you are hitting at the practice range. At most ranges, a small bucket is about the number of shots most duffers hit in a round. Why hit more?

Most importantly, with less golf balls to hit, you are more likely to take your time and focus on each shot. If you spend an hour at the range, then a small bucket comes to about a ball a minute. I suspect that most of us go through a large bucket in less time than that. With fewer balls to hit, you can take your time and make each one count.

Take twice as long. Now that you have fewer balls to hit, take your time between shots. This isn't a race. Most practice ranges have those trays next to the mat, so you can hit a ball, rake your next ball onto the mat, and hit again. One range I go to even has an automatic ball teeing system that puts the next ball on the tee after each shot, so you don't even have to rake the next ball onto the mat. Remember, the practice range owners want to make money, so the more balls you hit in a short period of time, the better. If they had the best interest of your golf game at heart, they would have you walk back to a ball dispenser between each and every shot to retrieve your next ball to hit. Take your time when you practice. Get off the mat between each shot, think about what you want to do on the next swing, take a practice swing, go through your preshot routine, then set up and hit the ball.

Have a strategy for the range. What do you want to work on when you go to the range? Pick one thing to practice, and practice that one thing. Do you want to hit your short irons straighter? How do you want to do that? What's your plan to hit your short irons straighter? Unfortunately, the behavior of most golfers at the practice range is a study of how poor practice strategies lead to poor results. Most of us mindlessly select clubs to hit, make either no adjustments or multiple adjustments between each swing, never learn anything constructive from the last swing, and generally go about the business of screwing up our swings on the practice range. Pick one part of your game to work on, devise a plan to work on this part of your game, and then stick to that plan.

Prepare yourself physically for the driving range. How many people do you see on the range that stretch and warm up before they start hitting balls at the range? If they do, they usually look embarrassed to be doing so and rush through the process. I suppose we don't want everyone else to know that we are old and out of shape—as if they won't figure that out after they see a couple of shots. Spend five minutes stretching and taking some slow, relaxed practice swings before hitting the first ball. Whatever you do for your usual warm-up prior to round of golf should be your warm-up on the practice range.

Start with your best. Hopes are high, but confidence is fleeting for most duffers on the practice range. Before working on an area of weakness, hit five or ten shots with your shortest favorite club. Start with a few half or three-quarter swings and then a few full swings. It is common to see people on the range start with their driver. Unless that's the best club you hit, you should only hit your driver at the range if that's the part of your game that you planned to work on. I know some people call the practice range a "driving range," but we'd all be better off if the other name for the practice range was the "chipping and pitching range." Start with the club you are most comfortable swinging, and when you feel confident in your basic swing, shift to the area of weakness you want to work on.

Focus on your *practice.* We've all done it. We go to the range with the intention of working on pitch shots, and then the golfer in the next station starts booming drives into the net at the back of the range. "Driver distance envy" kicks in, and we reach for the driver and begin flailing at the ball. If this scenario sounds familiar, then stop and realize that you are trying to impress people you don't know and will probably never see again. Focus on your practice, put the driver back in the bag, and work on what you planned to work on.

Set a realistic goal. Let's say you want to improve your accuracy from 150 yards. If you're a high handicapper, then sticking it within twenty feet every time is probably an unrealistic goal. Instead, focus on minimizing your worst mistakes. If you slice the ball to the right, define success as any shot that is less than thirty feet right of the pin, even if it is sixty feet left of the pin. If you tend to hit the ball fat, define success as anything, regardless of direction, that is not fat even if you top the ball and hit a worm burner. Golf is a game of "acceptable mistakes." Allow yourself the mistakes that you can live with on the course and focus on minimizing the shots that put you in serious trouble.

Picture a typical hole. Most golfers believe that they hit the ball better on the practice range than on the course. Actually, most of us hit the ball about the same in both places, but it just seems like we hit it better at the range. On the range, we get multiple "do-overs" and we have a memory bias that remembers the good shots and forgets the poor shots that would put us in an impossible situation if we were on the course. It is easy to ignore bad shots on a practice range. The practice range is a fantasy world of unlimited mulligans. The practice range also can be deceiving because it is so wide. The same shot that looks "just a little right" on the range is actually in the trees or lake on the right on a typical fairway.

You need to bring this practice range fantasyland back to reality. Picture a hole that you play regularly. If you are working on your drives, picture a fairway you play well. Where are the trees, bunkers, and rough? Where do you most not want to hit it, and where do you most want to hit it on this hole? If you are working on approach shots, picture a green that you can usually hit. This is not the time to picture the 12th at Augusta and get tied in knots. You want to picture a hole that you typically play and with which you have had some success. By doing so, you mentally narrow the practice range and put some realism into your practice.

Stop with your best. You want to end on a good shot or two, something that improves your confidence and gives your brain and body something good to remember and take from the range. Most of us hit every ball in the bucket, then look around to make sure nobody is looking and rake back the balls in front of us that we topped earlier. We desperately want to hit these last few balls well, put pressure on ourselves to end on a good note, and make it nearly impossible to do so. When you get to the last five of ten balls in your bucket, stop as soon as you hit two or three good shots and leave the rest of the balls for someone else. If you're the frugal type who simply can't bear to leave any balls unhit, then hit a few short chip shots with the remaining balls.

What if your swing is so screwed up that you don't hit any good shots as you are getting near the bottom of the bucket? Take a short break, pull back out your warm-up club (the one you started with) and hit a few three-quarter swing shots, focusing on making good contact, not on how far or straight the ball goes. At all costs, leave the practice range on an up note. You're not only working on technical skills; you're also working on improving your confidence, and you want to leave the practice range being more confident—not less—in your game.

Solidify your practice mentally. As you drive home from the range, what were the one or two swing keys that worked? Put a name to the physical sensation you are trying to replicate. When you are at the course, you can remind yourself of these keys during your preshot routine. Put a notebook in your golf bag and write down a couple of notes on what worked. For most of us, our memory isn't what it used to be. What we learned on the practice range can fade from memory fairly quickly. Many times I've played a half dozen holes before stumbling on a swing thought from my last practice. Of course, a third of my round didn't have the advantage of this brilliant insight. Take notes of what you learned on the practice range so you can review these swing keys before the round.

Flexibility and familiarity—two aspects to practice when not at the range

Golf is not the most physically demanding sport, especially when played with golf carts. Despite this, you do need to be in reasonable shape to play. Being stronger and in better cardiovascular shape will help, but the greatest improvement for most golfers comes from something that takes the least time to work on—flexibility. I realize that this is not typically considered part of the mental game of golf, but your mind has to have something with which to work. All the "picture yourself at the beach with the waves gently lapping in and new wave music playing in the background" relaxation training will not reduce your muscle tension much if you can't touch the back of your right shoulder with your left hand. Becoming more flexible is critical to maintaining a relaxed swing—more important than any form of relaxation strategy for the average duffer—and increased flexibility will increase your swing arc and swing speed as well.

Obtaining and maintaining flexibility is crucial to your swing. A few practice swings on the first tee will do little to improve your flexibility if you aren't stretching throughout the year. All it takes is five minutes every day or so to improve your flexibility and make it easier to loosen up and relax when you play. You can even stretch during commercials while watching TV. Since this is a book about the mental game, not physical preparation, and since physical fitness is not my area of expertise, check with the American College of Sports Medicine (ACSM) for instruction on proper stretching techniques. If you do some stretching exercises throughout the year, you'll find that it is much easier to stay relaxed on the course and to use relaxation strategies to keep tension from interfering with your swing. You'll also find that you hit the ball better and farther the more flexible you become.

Along with flexibility, developing familiarity with your basic grip, stance, and posture is something that you can practice nearly anytime or anywhere. How many times on a course have you taken your stance, gripped the club, and wondered how this alien object ended up in your hands? It's as if some form of golf amnesia has overtaken you. I won't cover Ben Hogan's five essential elements of the golf swing—I couldn't do them justice—but grip and stance are elements that are easily practiced at home. Keep a club at the office, or in the room in your house where you usually spend your time. The house is actually a great place to work on these elements because you have ready access to a mirror to check your grip and posture. From the mental perspective, it is important that the club feels like a part of you, and that your grip and stance feel natural. There is a lot to think about on the course. Grip, stance, and posture should be so comfortable that you need only a couple of quick checks in your preshot routine to make sure you are set up properly. If you are standing over the ball wondering about your grip or stance, no amount of relaxation training and mental imagery will make you feel comfortable.

Putting practice is also something you can do in the house and is a great way to keep your game sharp during the winter months. You can invest in a putting mat, but just putting to a spot on the carpet will do the trick. As with practicing grip and posture, the primary goal of putting practice in the house is to ensure that your putting grip, posture, and putting stroke feel natural when you get on the course. Of course, you also want to roll the ball into the make-believe hole on your carpet, but you mostly want the process of gripping your putter, taking your stance, and stroking the putt to feel automatic on the course.

Take it to the course

At the practice range,

1. Take your time and hit a small number of balls.
2. Plan what you will practice and stay focused on this plan.
3. Warm up and build confidence with your go-to club before working on the part of the game you want to improve.
4. Stop practicing when you feel good about your swing, not when the balls run out.
5. Take notes on what worked.
6. Whether or not you can make it to the range, take the time at home to stretch and make your grip and stance second nature, especially for putting.

Chapter 3

Pre-round Preparation

The battle cry of all card-carrying duffers is "Hurry up, our tee time is in fifteen minutes!" We search for our golf shoes, grab the clubs, jump in the car, and drive at breakneck speed to the course. When we arrive, we jump out, lace up our shoes, throw the golf bag on our shoulder, and run to the clubhouse. Then it's to the tee, a couple of hurried practice swings, and then swing out of our shoes with our driver on the first tee. And we wonder why our game sucks? The definition of good pre-round preparation for the typical duffer is having enough time to putt a few times and grab a beer before rushing off to the first tee.

Have you ever been to a professional tournament? Remember that these are the pros: people with exceptional skill and ability who golf every day for a living. They show up well before the round, hit some balls on the range, chip and pitch for a while, and spend significant time on the practice green. Then they take a break, get some water and maybe even a snack, and then go to the first tee with plenty of time to spare. And that doesn't include any of the time spent practicing after their round.

Now I know that most recreational golfers don't have time for this amount of preparation. We have obligations: spouses, children, work, and all manner of things that make us feel lucky if we can squeeze in a round of golf. We can't spend all day at the course like the pros do. With minimal planning, however, it is possible to develop a pre-round routine that not only shakes off the rust but also prepares us mentally for the round.

Give yourself a half-hour minimum at the course before your tee-time. You may not always be able to do this, but you need at least thirty minutes to unwind from your busy life and make the mental shift to playing golf. This is the first transition and one of the most important transitions you'll make—from your busy and often stressful life to playing golf. Some of my worst rounds have come from rushing out of the office early to squeeze in a round before dark. With no time to put the stress of work behind me and make the transition to a relaxed game of golf, I had the touch and feel of a gorilla for the first few holes. In hindsight, it would have been better to give myself a little time to unwind and prepare to play golf, even if I was not able to get in a full round before dark. Give yourself time to make the mental transition from your hectic life to playing golf.

Make putting your first pre-round practice priority. Nothing you do during your pre-round routine will improve your score more than practicing putting. Over a third of your strokes each round are putts, and you can usually groove an adequate putting stroke with just a few minutes of practice. More importantly, putting on the practice green provides you with a feel for the speed and break of the greens you will be playing that day. The confidence you develop from some pre-round putting practice can also spill over to the other aspects of your game. If you feel confident that you can two-putt once you're on the green and maybe even sink a couple of ten-to twenty-footers, you will take some pressure off the rest of your game.

But don't just putt around. Practice putting with a purpose and follow a regular putting practice routine. The following is one way to go about practicing putting before a round. You need to develop a routine that works for you.

1) Practice pace first and foremost. For the average duffer, poor putts are more likely due to poor pace than to poor line. We spend most of our time on the greens analyzing the break, but we'd be much better off spending most of our time gauging the speed. If you miss a putt by ten feet, it is much more likely that it was ten feet long or short than ten feet right or left. Focusing on pace will improve

your lag putting, reduce the chance of three-putting a green, and also improve your ability to sink breaking putts which depend as much on pace as on direction.

One way to practice pace while taking direction out of the equation is to putt to the fringe. Drop a few balls on the green and putt to the fringe on various sides of the green. Putting to the fringe allows you to practice putts of a variety of lengths and slopes, providing touch and pace for the greens you will be playing that day without focusing on the line of the putt.

Practicing pace without concern for the line also frees you up to gain a feel for the speed of the greens and ingrain the relationship between how fast you stroke the ball and how far it rolls. Focusing on the line of a putt often produces a cascade of mechanical stroke thoughts to keep the stroke and putter face square and on line. Such thoughts overwhelm the more intuitive feel for the pace of the putt. Develop a feel for putting speed first, and direction will follow.

2) Practice line. Having developed a feel for the pace of putts, you are now capable of getting most lag putts within a makeable range. Now your practice should turn to increasing your chances of sinking those makeable putts.

Start with a fairly straight flat or slightly uphill putt, paying attention to setting up on line and having the putter square to the line when it makes contact. Focus on putting the ball straight and true, and at a speed that goes beyond the hole. Putt from two to six feet uphill until you feel comfortable being able to sink these putts out on the course. Shouldn't you practice longer putts? If you have time, practicing putts up to ten feet or so may be helpful, but remember that the goal of this part of your putting practice routine is to roll the ball on the desired line with your putter, and you can achieve that goal putting the distances that you should expect to make the putt. Beyond six feet, even the pros have a drop off on percentage of putts made, and beyond ten feet, pace is probably more important than the line of your putt.

3) Practice breaking putts. If you are short on preparation time, practicing pace and line is probably adequate. If you have time, however, you may want to practice breaking putts of ten to fifteen feet,

especially if the greens are fast. Practicing breaking putts allows you to integrate your pace and line practice since a breaking putt requires a balance of pace and line.

Vary your speed and line on these putts (e.g. firm putt with less break vs. soft putt with more break) to help you visualize the break under different speeds. By varying the pace of breaking putts, you eventually develop a "crescent moon" visualization of a breaking putt that allows you to put the ball on the high line if putted softly and on the low line if putted firmly. Most golfers tend to underestimate the break and seldom miss above the hole, partly because it is difficult for them to see the high path to the hole. Once you've seen with your own eyes how far the ball can break and still have enough pace to make it to the hole, you are more likely to read these breaks well during the round.

You'll notice that nowhere in this sample putting practice routine is there an outcome goal (e.g., putt until you sink five putts in a row). Being too results-oriented and perfectionistic in your pre-round putting practice can produce additional tension and doubt before a round, especially if you don't meet these arbitrary outcome goals. You want to relax before the round. The primary result of pre-round putting practice should be to develop a feel for the pace of the greens and to develop confidence in your ability to putt on the line you select.

Short game practice

Chipping practice. If you have time to do more than putt before the round, hit a few practice chips. If this is not allowed on the practice green, then find a place where you can hit a few chips to a spot about twenty to thirty feet away. Set realistic goals for a duffer. The short game gurus emphasize the goal of chipping to within three feet. Although it would be great to get it this close to make an up-and-down, a realistic goal for most duffers is to get the ball on the green without wasting a stroke by chunking the chip shot. Therefore, the goal of hitting these few practice chip shots is simple—make solid contact and get the ball somewhere on the green. If it ends up close the pin, great. If it doesn't, you're still putting.

During your chipping practice, chipping the ball too far should always be an acceptable miss. Deceleration of the clubhead is a common cause of chunked chips (apologies for the alliteration), and deceleration is often the result of doubt and fear. As you take the club back, your mind begins the running commentary, *Is this too far back? I'm going to hit it too hard. It's going to fly across the green*, and your body adjusts to these thoughts by decelerating through the shot. When you practice chipping before a round, celebrate any shot that goes beyond the hole, even if it rolls off the other side of the green. Duffers more often hit a chip short versus long, so the acceptable miss is to chip beyond the pin. Aggressive chips are signs that you are beating doubt and fear and confidently accelerating the club through the ball.

Sand shots. One of the most under-practiced shots of recreational golfers is the sand shot. Given the lack of practice, it should be no surprise that the outcome of most sand shots is either (a) taking enough sand to bury a small animal and leaving the ball in the bunker, or (b) hitting it thin and having your playing partners diving for cover.

Unfortunately, practice facilities at most public courses don't have a practice sand bunker. If they do, be sure to take advantage of it and hit a few practice bunker shots. Again, the goal of this practice should be simple—get out of the bunker. Focus on getting a feel for the sand and the sensation of hitting a sand shot that slices through the sand underneath the ball. Hitting just a few decent sand shots during your pre-round practice will increase your confidence in these shots during the round.

Pre-round practice range

Hitting balls on the practice range before a round often does more damage to a duffer's psyche than any other pre-round activity. Although practice of any kind is usually beneficial, the approach that most golfers take to hitting practice balls before the round is doomed to produce failure on the course. If going to the practice range is generally a good thing, then why is time on the practice range just before a round usually not a good idea?

First, most golfers are usually rushing to squeeze in this practice before their tee time. Rushing this practice time produces tension and compromises the swing. Bad swings and bad results feed off each other, quickly making a reasonable swing an absolute mess before the round begins. Unless you have plenty of time, it is best to skip the practice range altogether before a round.

Second, the practice range is not a litmus test of how well you will score in the upcoming round. Since these practice shots are usually the first swings of the day, usually with insufficient warm-up, they are also usually not the best swings of the day. Practice shots prior to the round must be made with low expectations. How many times have you left the practice range with more doubt about your swing than you had when you started? Unless you have a routine that leaves you feeling better about your swing at the end than at the beginning of these practice range shots, then it is better not to hit practice range shots.

Third, time at the practice range before a round is not the time to fix your swing. The swing you brought to the course is the swing that you will have for the round. Working on your swing at the practice range will only serve to give you more swing thoughts than you need. If you do go to the practice range before the round, then use the practice to ingrain the one or two swing keys you developed in prior practice. Use the pre-round practice mostly to determine how you are hitting the ball that day and use this information to adjust your strategy during the round. If you find on the practice range that your shots are leaking to the right, better to adjust to that during the round than to try with only a few practice swings to straighten out your shot.

So what should you do on the practice range before a round? First, go to the range only if you have enough time to also do the putting and short game practice. Second, do all your pre-round stretching and warm-up before hitting the first range ball. Third, focus your practice on (a) making solid ball contact, (b) internalizing swing keys, and (c) getting a sense of the swing you brought to the course. Let's take each one separately.

Solid ball contact. For the typical recreational golfer, the only crucial task of hitting a few range balls before the round should be to get a good feel for solid ball contact. If you think about it, the shot that causes you the most strokes as a duffer is the fat shot—hitting ground before ball. Therefore, take an iron you feel comfortable hitting, use a three-quarters swing, and focus on hitting the ball first. To help with this focus and save practice tee turf at the same time, do what the pros do. Put your ball just behind a divot and hit the shot so your club goes through the same divot over and over again, taking only a thin sliver of grass each time. Also, allow thin shots to be okay. To work on making solid contact and not hit the ball fat, you need to give yourself an acceptable miss. Therefore, if you cut the ball in half, that's okay—at least you didn't hit it fat.

Internalize swing keys. The pre-round practice range is not the time or place to analyze your swing or develop a new swing key. It is the time to internalize a swing key that you have been working on. In other words, you want to translate this mental instruction into a physical sensation. If your swing key is to shift your weight to your front foot in the downswing, you want to feel yourself doing this and commit that feeling to memory by rehearsing it. By the end of practice, you want any swing thought to be associated with a physical sensation you can reproduce. If you leave the practice range with a list of mechanical thoughts to remember on the course, you can bet that your round will be miserable. Stick with "one thought, one feel," and you have half a chance to improve your round.

Today's swing. Everybody's swing differs from round to round. The higher your handicap, the more your swing will differ each round. You want to use any pre-round practice time to see what ball flight you can expect for the round. If you are consistently pulling shots left, you will want to adjust your target areas to the right during the round, especially when there is trouble left. The pre-round practice should be used to adjust your course strategy for the swing you brought to the course, not to fix your swing. Instead of becoming frustrated by the poor shots on the practice range, use it to know what strengths and weaknesses you are bringing to your round and plan accordingly. If you are not hitting long irons solid, then you know to choke down on the 5-wood or lay up with a shorter club rather than risk using long-iron shots during the round.

I realize that the advice to avoid the practice range before a round is counter to most of what you have heard or seen, but this is one of the mental game differences between pros and duffers. The skill of pros allows them to make fine adjustments to the swing on the practice range before a round. More importantly, they can make these adjustments as needed and leave the practice range with the confidence to hit nearly any shot during the round. The typical recreational golfer, however, is actually more likely to make an adjustment that makes their swing worse instead of better. If you hit shots well on the practice range, then you would probably also have hit them equally well on the first few holes, so the practice range doesn't buy you much. If, however, you hit them poorly, you leave the range with less confidence and even less of an idea of how to put a good swing on the ball. If you have the time, can keep your expectations low, and can use these pre-round practice range shots to learn what you should rely on during the round, then go to the practice range before the round. Otherwise, you are better off skipping the practice range before the round.

Take it to the course:

1. Give yourself plenty of time at the course before your round, at least a half hour.
2. Put a priority on practicing putting before the round, focusing primarily on pace.
3. If time permits, practice your short game, chips, and sand shots, with the goal of making good contact (with the ball or the sand) and landing the ball on the green.
4. Avoid the practice range before the round unless you have plenty of time and the right mindset for this practice.

Chapter 4

What Did You Expect? Setting Realistic Goals for Your Round

One of my old playing partners is an extremely good-natured soul, but a terrible golfer. Each time I picked him up to play, his wife would yell out as we left, "Break a hundred!" He would usually return a sarcastic "thanks." Funny thing is that I don't ever remember him breaking 100.

You may not be so fortunate to have a loving spouse who will set scoring goals for your round with the intent of pointing out the futility of such goals. Who came up with setting scoring goals anyway? Nearly every golfer has the goal of breaking 100 or 90 or 80. However, with the exception of 90, which is bogey golf, these 10-stroke scoring goals are arbitrary and are not associated with any real milestone.

More importantly, these 10-stroke increments are not equidistant. It is much easier to get from 110 to 100 than to get from 90 to 80. If you can hit the ball solidly most of the time, regardless of distance or direction, you can drop 10 strokes from 110 to 100 simply by staying focused during the round, playing conservatively, and minimizing blow-up holes. To move from 90 to 80, however, takes substantial improvements in the accuracy of approach shots and in the short game. Therefore, the first step in setting realistic goals is to throw out these arbitrary 10-stroke milestones. To set realistic goals for your round, you must first make a conscious decision to set a goal for the round. Although this sounds obvious, many golfers start their round with either no goal or a "brain-dead" goal that is poorly considered. Just because you managed to break 90 last week doesn't mean that should be your goal this week. A number of factors should affect your goals for the round.

a) The course: Have you played the course before? How long is it? How tight is it? What's the stroke rating? What's the slope rating? Does the course fit your game or not? Pros expect different scores on a US Open course than they do on a typical tour course. With much more variability in your game than the pros, you should expect your scores will differ even more from the easier to harder courses you play.

b) The conditions: If it is windy or cold or raining, you should lower your scoring expectations for the round. More importantly, these conditions will affect some golfers differently. If it is windy and you hit high fades, you can expect your scores to be more adversely affected than your partner who tends to hit low draws. Lowering your expectations in difficult conditions is not the same as giving up. Windy, rainy conditions can be a great test of your game and your mental approach, but if you typically shoot 90 in good conditions, then shooting 99 in windy conditions is still an ambitious goal.

c) The context: Most duffers understand that the course and conditions can influence your score for a round, but what about the situation in which you are playing? Are you with your regular playing partners and can focus on your game, or are you playing with yahoos who are distracting and irritating? Are you playing with others who play at around your skill level and pace, or are you out with family or friends who are just learning the game? Are you there simply to play golf, or do you have other agendas such as business or socializing? Even if you are the type who can shift focus well, the people you are playing with and the reason you are playing with them can affect your round.

Be honest with yourself. If the purpose of playing a round is to hang out with friends and drink a few beers while enjoying being outside and not working, then that's your goal. The chance that you can joke around with friends, have a few beers, *and* also have the best round of your life is infinitesimally small. If you are serious about scoring well on the course, then minimizing your alcohol intake and having playing partners also serious about scoring well increases your chances. If your playing partners are not taking the round seriously, it will be difficult for you to score well. There's nothing wrong with deciding that your round is about having fun with friends, but if that's the primary goal, then you need to adjust the expectation for your score accordingly.

The pace of play also can affect your round. If it looks like this will be one of those "Bataan Death March" rounds, then lower your expectations for the round a bit since you will find it more difficult to keep your rhythm and focus over a six-hour round.

After considering the factors that will affect your goals for the round, set your goals for shots and holes as well as for the round. In addition to setting unrealistically high goals, most golfers also focus exclusively on the score for the entire round as their goal. Having a goal only for the round makes it too easy to give up on the goal. Let's say you decide that you are breaking 90 today and playing along well until the wheels come off on a hole. After that snowman (8) on a par four, you figure the goal is lost for the day and the rest of the round no longer matters. Actually, the 8 only contributes 4 of the 18 strokes over par that you gave yourself that day (less than 25 percent), but the goal is still likely to feel impossible to achieve.

Until you are a single-digit handicapper, I would argue that you should never set a score for the round as your goal. If you feel you must, then set the score realistically and in smaller steps of improvement than ten-stroke increments. If you think about dividing the round in thirds (six holes each), then the scores below are reasonable increments for making improvements on the same course under similar conditions. As the course and conditions change, your goals should be adjusted according. Also remember that attainment to each lower score will take more time and skill development to achieve than the last.

108: Double bogey for each hole.

102: The equivalent of double bogey on twelve holes, bogeys on six holes.

96: Bogeys on twelve holes, double bogeys on six holes.

90: Bogey golf.

84: Bogeys on twelve holes, pars on six holes.

78: Bogeys on six holes, pars on the rest.

72: Par golf.

Setting the goal for the round based on these milestones gives you some sense how to set your goal for the holes on the course. If you usually shoot over 90, set a goal for how many holes of bogey or better you want to shoot today. If you usually shoot around or under 90, then set a goal for how many holes of par or better you want to shoot today. Each hole now becomes the focus of your game, and one blow-up hole doesn't ruin your game. Even after that snowman 8 on the last par four, you still have your goal for the number of bogeys or better this round. Forget the score for the round and instead focus on the number of bogeys or pars you want. You'll find that you play better and score better.

You'll also notice that the goal for the number of par or bogey holes is positive, not negative. Telling yourself that you are not making any triple bogeys today sets you up to avoid something negative instead of achieving something positive, and once you've made your triple bogey or worse, your chance of achieving your goal is zero.

Focusing on the score for each hole also makes clear what you need to do to reach the scores for the round that you ultimately want to obtain. Ninety doesn't look as hard to achieve when you realize that you just need to bogey each hole. Trying to shoot par on each hole often contributes to bad rounds for most duffers. It's folly for a high handicapper to stand on the tee of a 400-yard par four with water on the right and think that you could make par with a good drive, long-iron approach, and two putts. If instead the goal is to make bogey, you can hit a three or five-wood safe down the left side, hit a short iron to a safe landing area, then hit a pitching wedge or chip onto the green. The hole doesn't seem as ominous anymore, and the goal you have set for yourself is in your reach.

As an example, suppose your scores are stuck in the 90s and you want to get your score below 85. Obviously, more practice and an improved short game will help, but ask yourself, "What will it take to score under 85?" All you have to do is shoot bogey golf on most holes and scrape together a half a dozen pars. Forget your score for a while and focus on reaching the goal of shooting par or better on six holes. What you will find is that each hole becomes important. You haven't blown your goal with one bad hole, and you don't have to "catch up" with pars or birdies to score well. You just need to find six pars on the course today.

Not only do your goals become more realistic and remain challenging throughout the round when you focus on the number of pars or bogeys you make each round, but you will find that your focus on each hole improves. From wherever you are on the course, including in the woods and hazards, you are always asking yourself how you can make par or bogey (or double bogey) from here. Around the green in regulation, you become focused on how to get up and down and not settle for a bogey because this could be one of your pars for the round. Basically, you find that you seldom give up on a hole when you focus on the number of pars or bogeys you want to get each round.

Suppose you're in the 100-plus club and even bogeys are not realistic, then shift to an even smaller mini-goal for your round. Focus on a goal for each type of shot for the round. Again, the focus needs to be positive, so you want to frame the goal as something you do, not something you avoid doing. At this level, the focus should be on solid contact above all else. Direction is secondary, and distance is not even a consideration. How many shots do you want to hit solid today? How many fairways do you want to hit (keep the goal liberal, so "hit" means anything not in the woods, on another fairway, or out of bounds)? Forget greens in regulation at this level; instead, set a goal for how many approach shots (regardless of how many shots occurred before it) end up around the green (within chipping distance). How many greens do you want to two putt today? Keep track of your shots that meet your goals and forget your score for now. When you stumble upon the realization that you are shooting below

110, then you can shift your goals to focus on the number of pars and bogeys for the round.

Whether you focus your goals for the round on score, holes, or shots, make sure that you set realistic goals that are a small improvement from your present performance. Take the course, conditions, and context into account and decide before the round what you want to focus on and what your goal will be for today's round. With realistic mini-goals, you'll find that you play better and enjoy yourself more.

I know that some of you are high drive types who have difficulty with the concept of lowering expectations. You believe that the reason you have achieved what you have in life is because you set tough and challenging goals that took long hours and hard work to achieve. That's great, and if you want to take the same approach of long hours and hard work to improve your golf score, then by all means, feel free to set high expectations. The typical recreational golfer I know, however, wants to achieve these high expectations without the long hours or hard work, and the mismatch leads to frustration and disappointment. Set realistic goals, gradually improve your game, and most importantly, enjoy playing golf again.

Take it to the course:

1. Set a realistic goal for your round taking into account the course, condition, and context in which you are playing.
2. Instead of setting a scoring goal for the entire round, consider other scoring goals like the number of pars or bogeys for the round.
3. If you are struggling during the round, focus your goal on strokes instead of holes (e.g., hitting it solid each time).

Chapter 5

The First Tee

The first tee jitters affect everyone to some degree. Even pros will tell you they fear hitting it in the parking lot to the right off the first tee at Augusta National. The first tee shot, however, does not hold world peace in the balance. Your personal demise does not depend on the outcome of that first shot. This first shot of the round carries more weight than it should. Objectively, all the shots in your round count the same. Why then is the first tee shot so pressure-packed?

The first tee jitters result from a combination of having minimal prior information to predict how we'll perform on this first shot and irrational expectations of what this first shot means. In our minds, we make the first shot the most important, a critical symbol to our partners and anyone watching that we know how to play golf. As a result, the first tee shot carries more weight when we're playing with people we haven't played with before. We want to make a good impression and not have them think they got paired up with some hacker. Of course, the more pressure we put on ourselves to make a good impression with the first tee shot, the more likely it will go badly.

The first tee shot is also a sign to ourselves of how our round will go. We feel we have to get off to a good start. If we hit it badly, then thoughts about how badly our round will be start to creep in. If we hit it well, we feel more relief than we probably should because there are still 90 or 100 more strokes out there that we haven't hit yet. Combine the pressure of these first tee expectations with the fact that we don't have any previous shots from the round to use to predict how we'll play, and you have a recipe for tension and anxiety—high perceived stakes and low predictability.

To reduce the first tee jitters, you need a first tee preparation routine that relaxes you, reduces the importance of the first shot, and uses your memory of past rounds to improve predictability.

Relaxing for the first tee shot. Assuming you haven't hit balls on the practice range, this is the time to stretch and warm up. Don't cut short your stretching time. In addition to preventing injury and improving your golf swing flexibility, stretching will do more to help you relax than just about any other pre-round routine.

After stretching, go through a routine for gradually building your swing as you warm up. If you don't have such a routine, develop one. Full bore practice swings typically produce more tension, not less. Instead of swinging out of your shoes, these warm-up swings should start small and build gradually. For example, start with little half swings with your feet together and gradually increase the arc as you spread your feet apart. This is not a time to "think" about your swing. You are simply warming up your swing motion and developing the rhythm for your swing. This should be one of the most relaxing experiences of the day for you.

To help with relaxing, this is a good time to introduce deep breathing relaxation. With only a few deep breaths from your diaphragm (the muscle below your lungs), you can induce a state of relaxation while you warm up. The trick is to breathe slowly and from your abdomen. This means that your abdomen should expand as you breathe in, deflate as you breathe out. Most people try to relax by taking a deep breath, sucking in their abdomen, and expanding their chest. Unfortunately, this actually makes your breathing less full and deep, and also uses more muscles than needed.

Above all else, don't rush your warm-up time on the first tee. Even if you are late getting to the first tee and are the first one up in your group, take the time to warm-up. If you feel like you'll hold others up, let them hit first. The warm-up period on the first tee is one of the first of many transitions that you need to make during the round. It shifts you from not playing golf to playing golf. Give yourself the time to put your regular life behind you and focus on playing golf for the next few hours.

Mentally preparing for the first tee shot. Unrealistic expectations feed much of the tension we feel on the first tee. One source of tension is concern about what our playing partners will think of us based on this first shot. *What if I top it? What if I whiff it? What will these people think about me? I bet they'll think "who paired us up with this bozo?"* These types of thoughts are particularly prevalent when we are playing with people we want to impress, but with whom we have never played golf before (e.g., new client, new boss, new father-in-law), but they also can occur when playing with total strangers. Even among our regular playing partners, these thoughts about what others might think of us can slip in.

Not only do we try to impress others with the first tee shot, but we also try to impress ourselves. Some of the pressure we feel on the first tee is related to a belief that the first tee shot is a sign of how well we'll play during the round. Of course, this makes no sense. We don't use our performance during the first five minutes of work as a sign of how well work will go that day. Recreational golfers are so erratic that the first tee shot has almost no relationship to any other shot during the round anyway.

Fortunately, since we are the ones putting this pressure on ourselves, we can also take it away. Others will probably think we hit a bad first tee shot when we hit a bad tee shot, but it's unlikely anyone will conclude we are a bad golfer or a bad person based solely on our first tee shot. And if they did, why would we give their misguided opinion any weight? For the recreational golfer, the first tee shot is just one of the 100 or so strokes we'll make during the round. A poor drive on the first tee will cost a stroke or two, but we've wasted many more strokes than that in a typical round. Keep your expectations in check.

To increase the predictability of your first tee shot, visualize good tee shots from your previous round. This is particularly easy to do if you've played the course before and can recall other first tee shots that you've hit well. There is no need to visualize or remember the best tee shots, just the ones that were solid and in play. Recalling these tee shots will give you greater confidence in your ability to hit a serviceable tee shot on the first hole.

Play conservative on the first tee. The paradox of the first tee shot is that despite the anxiety and lack of confidence about this shot, recreational golfers often make this one of their more aggressive shots. The tendency is to pull out the driver and try to hit the first tee shot as far as possible. Why does the first tee shot need to be a booming drive? It's probably because we are trying to prove to ourselves how good we are going to be today. The first tee shot ends up often being both our most fearful and most hopeful shot of the round, and both expectations are unrealistic.

Be relaxed and confident, but also be conservative on the first tee. Look at the fairway, disregard distance, and look for the safest place to hit your tee shot. This should be the widest part of the fairway with the least trouble. If there is trouble in play at 190 yards on the right, then a shot shorter than 190 yards that favors the left side is the best shot, even if that leaves you 180 yards to the green for your second shot. If the first hole is a dogleg, this is not the time to cut the corner. Instead, target the wide landing area on the opposite side of the dogleg. The approach shot will be longer than you might like, but it will still be an approach shot instead of a punch shot out of the woods.

And unless your driver is the club you are the most comfortable hitting, use a 3 or 5-wood instead off the first tee. Actually, most duffers should just keep the driver in the trunk of their car when they play a round, but for heaven's sake, don't pull it out on the first tee unless you feel confident with your driver. Hit the club you are most comfortable hitting—the one with which you will make solid contact with the ball. If that is a 7 iron, hit it. Two good 7 irons will get you within pitching distance of most par fours. If recreational golfers were offered the chance to record a bogey and skip the first hole, most would take it and run. Yet the swing on the first tee looks more like someone trying to make a birdie than a bogey. Dial down your ambitions on the first tee, play conservative, and hit the club you hit solid most of the time.

Take it to the course

1. Make a relaxing transition from not playing golf to playing golf by taking the time to warm up on the first tee.
2. Keep your expectations in check. The first tee shot is only one of the 90 to 110 strokes you'll make during the round. Visualize good tee shots from your previous round and use those memories to instill confidence in your first tee shot.
3. Be conservative. Hit the shortest and safest drive you can on the first hole.

Chapter 6

Transitions after a Bad Shot

Making the transition from one shot to the next is one of the most important mental skills a recreational golfer—or any golfer for that matter—can learn. Think about the times you have executed a shot while still thinking about the last shot. One sign of someone who has not mastered shot transition is the "mad swing," a flailing overswing at the ball caused by still stewing about the last shot or hole. Another sign of not mastering shot transition is when a great shot is followed by a terrible one because you want to take advantage of the great shot you just hit. That's why the first task at hand prior to any preshot routine is to make a clean mental transition from the last shot to the next shot, especially when the last shot was bad.

Nobody can be emotionless on the golf course. Bad shots are going to frustrate you and produce negative emotions and physical tension. Actually, even great shots may produce tension because of the pressure you may place on yourself on the next shot. Feeling like you need to take advantage of a great drive can introduce as much tension as recovering from a bad shot. All of us have had that experience. We hit a great drive and follow it by laying the turf over the approach shot, partly because we put pressure on ourselves to make good use of the great drive that came before.

When you hit a bad shot, stifling your emotions isn't the answer. Your last shot sucked, you know it sucked, you are in significant trouble on the hole because you put a poor swing on the ball, and you can't do anything about it now. Ticks you off, doesn't it? You may want to act like it is okay, but deep inside you know it is not. Unless you are just out for a stroll and don't really care about how you play, then you are going to experience negative emotions on the golf course. Welcome to the human race. Ignoring these feelings will only serve to allow tension to creep into your swing. Unless you are great at compartmentalizing your emotions, your frustration will sneak out when you don't expect it, and overreactions to minor screwups will begin to occur.

It also isn't advisable to "channel" your frustration into your next shot. With some sports, you can use your frustrations to improve your performance. In football, you might be able to channel your frustration about missing one play by playing more aggressively on the next play. Unfortunately, adrenaline and tension are not aids to a golf swing, especially for duffers. You need to manage your emotions between shots. To manage your emotions between shots, you must (a) reduce your expectations about each golf shot to a reasonable level, (b) manage the experience of what you feel after the shot, (c) shift to reviewing your swing fundamentals, and (d) redirect focus to the next shot.

Expectations. Nothing will keep your emotions under control after a shot better than managing your expectations before the shot. If you expect a perfect shot every time, you will be disappointed on nearly every shot. Very few shots actually make sweet contact and fly exactly where you wanted them to go. Consider your skill level and how you are hitting the ball today. What would be a *realistic* outcome for this shot? For most duffers, solid contact and a ball that goes in the general direction you wanted it to go is a realistic expectation for the shot. Anything more than that is nice, but certainly not expected.

I must admit that this was one of the worst areas of my mental game for most of my golf life. As a card-carrying perfectionist, I was often frustrated or disappointed by any shot that did not turn out exactly as envisioned. If I wanted the ball to fade a bit and it went straight, even though it was hit well and still near the target, I would get frustrated that it didn't go off as planned. Any missed putt inside twenty feet was frustrating, even though, like nearly all golfers including the pros, I miss most putts outside of ten feet. Fortunately, an old playing partner and psychologist colleague turned around my unrealistic expectations on the golf course. After I would hit anything less than perfect shot, he would always say "good miss." A "good miss?" How could "good" and "miss" be used together in the same sentence? A miss, by definition, is a bad event. But what he would eventually convey to me with this phrase was that the shot wasn't perfect, but it was good enough. The shot was good enough to still have a chance at bogey or par or even birdie. The swing also wasn't perfect, but it was good enough that I didn't have to spend the rest of the round in some internal golf clinic hell trying to fix my swing. I could tweak my swing as needed, but it was good enough to get me through the round. After a while, the concept of a "good miss" began to sink in and became a part of my preshot routine. Standing over the ball, my main consideration is what shot is "acceptable," good enough to give me a chance at par or bogey on that hole. As long as I hit the shot that is good enough, I'm happy.

Some people fear reducing their expectations because they think they won't strive as hard to be better. First, we are not talking about having any expectations, just more realistic ones. Second, even if you put your best effort into reducing your expectations, you would probably still have them higher than necessary to stay motivated to improve your game. Third, beating up on yourself is not an effective strategy for getting better at golf, or most other things for that matter. If setting realistic expectations feels too foreign to you, then start by just experimenting with it. Go out for one round and set your expectations for each shot as low as you can reasonably set them. Any drive inside the tree line and over 150 yards is good. Any approach shot that is within twenty yards of the green is good. Any chip or pitch that lands on the green is good. Any putt that is within five or six feet of the cup is good. You'll find that you play just as well, if not better, with these realistic expectations than with your more perfectionistic ones.

In addition to managing your emotions, keeping your expectations realistic also improves your mental strategy during the game. With unrealistic expectations, most duffers try shots even the pros would not attempt. You just hit a high slice into the woods on the right, but now you are going to hit a low draw between two trees and carry the ball 200 yards to the green. What are you thinking? With a bucket of balls, you couldn't hit one low draw 200 yards on the practice range, much less between two trees. Keep your expectations realistic for each shot, and you will hit less ill-advised—otherwise known as stupid—shots and also manage your emotions better on the course.

Experience and manage emotions. Even with realistic expectations, you will hit some shots that will produce a negative emotional response. You planned on hitting the ball 50 yards left of the water hazard but somehow managed to put a swing on the ball that sliced it right in the lake. Now that shot sucked! No amount of managing your expectations can prevent an emotional response. This is the time for a few, well-chosen curse words. Cussing and other verbal expressions of emotion are always preferable to physical acts of violence to your clubs, yourself, or others. Your playing partners might be entertained by a good but infrequent tirade, but will not be happy if they have to duck for cover from a flying club.

To keep the emotional response reasonable, however, you want to watch out for personalizing and catastrophizing. Personalizing refers to the tendency to take the shot personally. Phrases like "you stupid idiot," and "what the hell am I doing playing golf" are examples of personalizing a bad shot. The bad shot has nothing to do with your intellect, personality, manhood (or womanhood), or character. You hit a bad shot. It doesn't mean you are a bad person. It doesn't even mean you are a bad golfer. It means you hit a bad shot. Telling yourself, "Now that shot sucked," is actually a positive mental strategy. First, it is the shot that sucked, not you. Secondly, it only sucked *now* and is therefore not a sign of some deep underlying flaw you have as a golfer. It was a mistake.

Catastrophizing is a fancy way of saying "making a mountain out of a molehill." Nothing that occurs during a round of golf has any serious or long-term consequences. There aren't thousands of dollars riding on a putt, just a $2 Nassau at best. World peace and prosperity do not hang in the balance. The Battle of Normandy was critical; golf is just a game. At the end of the round, you throw away your scorecard, go on with your life, and return to play again. Put the bad shot in perspective. The drive that went into the lake has cost you one stroke. You're hitting three and still have an outside chance at par, certainly at bogey. The terrible shot that put you in the water hazard cost you the same as a short putt that lipped out. Don't make a bad shot more than it is, and you will keep your emotional responses balanced, making the transition to the next shot easier.

Review Fundamentals. Some people simply must analyze their swing during the round. Although nothing is probably worse for your swing than thinking about it during a round, if you must analyze your swing after a bad shot, keep it short and simple. First, make sure that you have problem worth correcting. Some bad shots are produced by only a slight variation of a good swing. Unless you repeat the same bad shot over and over, you probably don't have a problem worth correcting. Make sure that you hit the same bad shot two or three times before you do anything. Second, the diagnosis must be obvious to you. If immediately after a bad shot, you know that shot (i.e., you have a long and personal relationship with that shot and what you do that usually produces it), then you have a chance to make a reasonable correction. If, however, you are standing there trying to figure out what went wrong, then all bets are that you will probably come up with the wrong problem and surely will come up with the wrong solution. You might identify a flaw in your swing, but it probably has nothing to do with what produced the bad shot in the first place. If you do make a swing correction, make it a simple, single key correction. If you tell yourself that you need to do *x and* do *y,* then you are likely to hit a different bad shot from trying to change too many things at once, and also won't know if it is *x* or *y* that produced the new bad shot or a better shot.

Instead of analyzing your swing after a bad shot, review the fundamentals of your swing before hitting the next shot. Develop your own checklist based on the bad habits that you know you get into.

Check your grip, your posture, your takeaway, your weight shift, or whatever aspects of your swing tend to be your well-worn problems. Reestablish your fundamentals and take a few practice swings before you put the club back in the bag after a bad shot. Doing this will reestablish your confidence and reduce the chance of repeating the problem. Again, this analysis is only recommended if you simply cannot stop yourself from analyzing your swing. If you can, the best response to a bad shot is to brush it off as an aberration and move on to the next shot.

Shift focus to the next shot. After managing your expectations and emotions from a bad shot, and after reviewing your swing fundamentals if you must, it is time to shift from the last shot to the next shot. It is best to end your focus on the last shot when you put the club back in the bag. Having a shift point—such as putting the club back in the bag—to mark the end of your thoughts and feelings about the last shot helps make the transition easier. It also allows you to enjoy the walk or ride with your playing partners to the next shot.

If you simply must ruminate about the last shot for a while longer, then feel free to ruin your walk or ride down the fairway while you beat up on yourself a little more. Some shots are so bad that they deserve a little more anguish than is possible before putting your club back in the bag. Make sure, however, that you have a good shift point before you begin your shot preparation for the next shot. The best way to ensure that you will hit another bad shot is to still be thinking about it when you are preparing for the next shot. If you are riding, don't get out of the cart until you are ready to focus on the next shot. If you are walking, don't set your bag down or take your hand off the pull cart until you are ready to focus on the next shot.

This transition from a bad shot to the next shot is one of the most challenging aspects of the mental game, and also one of the most important transitions if you want to play golf well. If you take away only one piece of advice to work on from this book, make it to improve your post and preshot routines to transition well from a bad shot to the next shot.

Transitions on and around the green. The area where it is most difficult to make a good transition between shots is around the green.

In the fairway, you have the time between shots to settle down from a poor shot and focus on the next. On and around the green, however, if you hit a bad chip or putt, you are usually still the next to play and others are waiting on you. In this situation, it is easy to feel the pressure to rush the next shot, so you hit a bad chip, walk five feet, and then quickly hit another bad chip. Most of the time, you are still using the same club to hit another bunker shot, another chip, or another putt.

Sand shots are an excellent example of this problem. You hit a sand shot that doesn't get out of the bunker and rolls back. You only have to take a few steps with the same club in your hand to hit your next shot. Frustrated and rushed, you swear to yourself that the next shot will get out of the bunker, and you airmail the next shot over the green.

Effectively transitioning between shots on and around the green is especially important, not only because the time to make these transitions is so short, but also because the shots on and around the green are so valuable to scoring well. Blow-up holes occur around the green. The *Xs* on the scorecard are not because it took us 10 strokes to get around the green, but because we left the ball in bunker, then hit it over the green, then chipped it thirty feet past the hole, then 3-putted from there.

Stay in place after a bad shot around the green. If you hit a bad chip or a bad putt, stay where you are for a few seconds to take a deep breath and prepare to leave the bad shot behind. The bad pitch, chip, or putt is so embarrassing that I think we just want to hit the next shot as quickly as possible to end the black cloud of a bad shot that lingers overhead. Maybe if we hit again quickly enough, our playing partners won't notice that the last shot sucked as much as it did. Stay put and don't move to your next shot until you are ready to leave that shot behind. Even if your next shot requires the same club, get the club's grip out of your hands. Carry the club holding the shaft or head. Balance it on your head if you must, but whatever you do, don't keep your hands on the grip as you walk to the next shot. Take a deep breath and clear your head before you prepare for the next shot. Take your time preparing for the next shot, even if you are still up.

Thirty seconds won't slow anyone up and will give you enough time to settle down before you begin your preshot routine for the next shot. Stretch, wipe your hands with a towel, or toss an extra ball in your hands. Do anything that will fill time and give you the time to transition from a bad shot around the green.

Take it to the course

1. Set realistic expectations about the shot you are about to hit so you can better manage your emotions after a poor shot.
2. Give yourself permission to get angry after a bad shot, but set up a transition action (putting your club in the bag, or taking the next shot's club out of the bag) that will mark the point where you stop berating yourself for the last shot and focus on the next shot.
3. Limit personalizing and catastrophizing shots so you can manage your emotional response from a bad shot.
4. If you must engage in swing corrections during the round, focus on swing fundamentals and keep it simple.
5. Take the time to shift your focus from the last shot to the next shot, especially around the green.

Chapter 7

Strategy from the Tee Box

For most duffers, the strategy off the tee consists of grabbing the driver, teeing it up, and hitting it as far as we can. The tee shot requires much more strategy than that. The tee shot is where recreational golfers often take the most risk for the least gain. Duffers tend to be the most aggressive off the tee and become increasingly tentative and conservative as they get closer to the hole. The reverse is more likely to produce good scores. If you were more aggressive around the green and less aggressive off the tee, you would be in the fairway more and leave fewer putts short.

Seldom is a good score on a hole determined by the length of a drive, but many bad scores result from errant drives that were driven farther than necessary. "Farther than necessary" is a foreign concept to most duffers. If we don't hit our tee shot as far as humanly possible, our playing partners will think we are wimps. Duffers play golf as if the goal of the game is to hit the ball as far as possible instead of as infrequently as possible. Choosing less distance off the tee is a difficult course management strategy to achieve because everyone "oohs" and "aahs" over long, booming drives, but remains deafly silent when we hit a short but safe shot. If you are playing to impress your playing partners, don't expect to score well.

The goal of the tee shot on a par four is to give yourself the best chance to hit the green on your next shot. How many yards away do you need to be to have a chance at hitting the green in regulation?

To answer this question, you need to know your maximum, minimum, and preferred approach shot yardages. What's the longest club you can hit fairly straight, and how far do you hit it? It could be a five-iron, but it could also be your three-wood if you hit it well. This is your maximum approach distance, and you need to get your tee shot at least within that distance to have a shot at the green. Being comfortable with this maximum approach distance gives you a lot more freedom on the tee. Let's say your maximum approach is 170 yards. On a long par four—say 400 yards—you need to hit a 230-yard drive to get within your maximum approach distance, but on a typical par four of, say 350 yards, you can hit a tee shot only 180 yards and be within your maximum approach distance.

Your medium or preferred distance approach shouldn't be 150 yards just because that is where they put the yardage marker. What is your best club from the 100 to 150 yard range? Closer is not always better. One of my playing partners can't hit his irons very well, but has a seven-wood that he can hit 160 yards straight nearly every time. Why would he ever want to be any closer to the green than 160 yards? On a 320-yard hole, his best strategy is to hit the seven-wood twice.

Your minimum distance approach is usually the distance of your full swing pitching or gap wedge. Notice that I didn't say sand or lob wedge. For most duffers, the bounce on the sand wedge is too great to make consistent solid contact off the fairways, especially hard fairways. The loft is too great on a lob wedge for most duffers to hit it a consistent distance. Even a small deviation from square will produce wide variability in distance. Unless you are one of the few duffers that can hit these more lofted clubs consistently, your best short-distance club is probably your pitching wedge. One of the most common strategic errors of recreational golfers is hitting their drive inside this minimum approach distance, especially on par fives. Even the pros, who are quite skilled with half and three-quarter shots, prefer to be a full swing distance from the hole. If you hit a full pitching wedge 100 yards, you want to hit your drive short enough that it puts you at least 100 yards out.

With this information about approach shot length in mind, you can now make an intelligent decision about how much you need to prioritize distance off the tee. For most duffers, the longer the hole, the more important distance is on the drive. On par fours over 400 yards, most duffers have the mindset that they must hit a long, booming drive to have a chance at par. I'm not sure why a 390-yard hole is okay, but a 410-yard is long, but that "4" in front of the other two numbers seems to have considerable influence on the tee strategy of most duffers. For a 400-yard hole, if you know that your maximum approach shot distance is 175 yards, then you know that you need a 225-yard drive to give yourself an approach shot—anything longer is gravy.

Knowing your maximum approach distance also helps you know when it is futile to try to go for the green in two. If your maximum approach distance is 180 yards, your good drives go 225 yards at most, and the hole is 420 yards…well, you do the math. There is essentially no chance that you will put together two shots that will get you on the green in regulation. In this situation, you're better off playing the hole as a par five and laying up to your short approach distance on your second shot.

Knowing your maximum, preferred, and minimum approach distances also influences your strategy off the tee. For a tight but short dogleg, there is no need to cut the corner. You can play the ball away from the corner and still have a good approach shot, and your preferred approach distance may be on the opposite side of the fairway from the corner of the dogleg.

If trouble comes into play at around a distance where your drives land, then knowing your approach distances can help you decide if you should be aggressive off the tee or lay back. Let's say there's a creek that comes into play on the right side of the fairway around 180 yards out. If the hole is 400 yards, then you may decide it is worth it to hit it long down the left side and flirt with the possibility of your ball going in the creek. But if the hole is 325 yards, then you can lay up off the tee short of the creek and still have a reasonable approach shot.

Plan your tee shot. The first step toward having a solid strategy off the tee is to look at the hole from the tee before you grab your driver. The tee shot strategy routine of most recreational golfers is to pull up to the tee in the cart, take a quick swig of beer, grab the driver, and march to the tee box of a hole they have never seen before. Take the time to stand at the tee without a club in your hand and determine your strategy first. After knowing how long the hole is and your approach distances, determine where on the fairway your maximum, minimum, and preferred approach distances are. Determine if the distances to bunkers and hazards will affect the distance you want to hit the tee shot. Also determine how tight or wide the fairway is. The tighter the fairway, the more you want to give up distance for accuracy. This is a novel concept for most duffers, but hitting your tee shot as long as possible is not always the best tee shot. You need to have some idea of how long you want to hit it and how much of a premium distance is for the hole.

Next, determine where you want to hit it. I know the center of the fairway seems like a logical answer, but often it is the wrong answer. Which side of the fairway has less potential trouble? From which side of the fairway is your best approach to the green? On well-designed courses, these two considerations are frequently at odds. The safer side of the fairway is also often the less preferred side from which to hit the approach shot. Golf architects can be devilish, can't they? For the typical recreational golfer, hitting a safe tee shot is preferable to setting up the best approach angle. Therefore, when in doubt, choose the safe side of the fairway.

Now that you have a plan for distance and direction, choose the club that will give you the distance you want the tee shot to go. Then tee the ball opposite the side of the fairway you want to favor to give you a better angle to that side. If you want the ball to go down the left side of the fairway, tee it up on the right side of the tee box. Finally, before going through your preshot routine, pick a target. In addition to picking a directional target such as a tree in the distance, you also want to picture where you want your ball to land on the line you have chosen. Now you have a plan for your tee shot that will increase your chances of hitting a safe and smart tee shot. Remember that golf is not a longest drive competition. The purpose of your tee shot is to put in position to approach the green—to turn a par four into an easy par three—and the best place to do that is from the fairway. Be conservative off the tee; there are plenty of opportunities to play more aggressively as you get closer to the green.

Tee shots on par fives. The strategy for tee shots on par fives is similar to the strategy on par fours. The primary difference, obviously, is that you are not usually planning to get to the green on your second shot. For most recreational golfers, the tee shot strategy for a par five should be not to go for the green in two. It is amazing to see the different thought processes of a golfer standing on a 460-yard par four versus a 460-yard par five. The same golfer who believes that the 460-yard par four is nearly impossible to reach in two also feels quite confident in his or her ability to reach the 460-yard par five in two. If it is too far for you to have a good chance to reach in two as a par four, it is also too far for you to have a good chance to reach it in two as a par five. If you are fortunate enough to hit a stellar drive on a par five and you find yourself within your maximum approach distance, then you may want to adjust your strategy and go for the green in two, but the sensible strategy from the tee box for all par fives should involve taking three shots to get on the green.

A common mistake of duffers on par fives is trying to hit a longer drive than normal because the hole is longer than normal. The "extra" shot on a par five is not the second shot, it's the first shot. All that you want to do on a par five tee shot is turn it into an easy par four. Par fives should be easy holes for most recreational golfers, but they often are the blow-up holes because there are more chances to hit stupid shots on par fives, beginning with the stupid shot off the tee.

Let's say that you are facing a longish par five of 550 yards. Even a short 200-yard drive now makes the hole a relatively short 350-yard par four. So you don't need to kill the drive, you just need to hit a reasonable drive in the fairway. "In the fairway" is the operative part of that phrase because most par fours don't have their tee boxes in the woods or in a water hazard. The tee shot strategy on a par five is not to hit it longer, but to hit it in the fairway. The best plan for most golfers is to pick the safest side of the fairway and hit the club that you can hit straight around 200 yards out. If you hit a fairway wood on every par five, you may find that you probably score better on these holes.

Even if the long drive mistake doesn't get you, the long second shot mistake usually will. After a good drive on a par five, most golfers want to hit it as far as they can for the second shot, often with disastrous consequences. Golf architects like to place the risk-reward challenges on a par five around the landing area of a long second shot, forcing players to decide if they want to play safely or risk the trouble of a longer second shot. Even if you hit a long second shot safely, you may now be inside your minimum approach shot distance and have to fashion a shot that you have little to no experience executing. Instead, treat your second shot on the par five just as you would your tee shot on the par four. Pick the best position and distance for your approach shot and hit it there. The only time most duffers should try to go for the green in two on a par five is when their second shots are within their maximum approach distance and there is little trouble around the green.

Stay focused on the second shot of a par five. Often, recreational golfers treat this shot casually with their only goal to advance the ball farther down the fairway. If you've hit a good tee shot in the fairway, this second shot should be treated the same as your tee shot strategy on a par four. Determine the distance and side of the fairway you want to hit the shot and focus on this landing area. A more casual, "hit it down the fairway" strategy can cause you to lose focus and hit an errant second shot. Stay focused and treat this shot as you would a par four tee shot.

By now you're probably saying, "You're taking all the fun out of the drive!" We all enjoy the thrill of smacking a long drive down the middle of the fairway. Nothing feels better than hitting it pure and long, particularly when we outdrive our playing partners. Unfortunately, the purpose of golf is not to hit the ball long; the purpose is to hit the ball as few times as possible. For the typical duffer, long is more often associated with being in trouble than being in the fairway. If you feel that playing conservatively off the tee takes the fun out of the game, then by all means, swing away and enjoy yourself. But if you do so, adjust your scoring expectations accordingly because you won't score as well as you will if you take a more conservative approach off the tee.

Take it to the course

1. Know your maximum, minimum, and preferred approach distances, and decide which club to hit off the tee based on these approach distances.
2. Plan your tee shot conservatively to minimize trouble and give you the best chance to hit the green in regulation.
3. On par fives, plan to take three stokes to get to the green, and make your tee shot strategy turning the par five into a short par four.
4. Use the same strategy for the second shot on a par five as you do for the tee shot on a par four—set yourself up for a good approach shot.

Chapter 8

"Get Out of Jail" Strategy

Before we deal with the strategy for the approach shot following a good drive, let's deal with the results of a bad drive that ends up in trouble. I realize that this seldom happens to you, but appease me.

One of the more noticeable differences between pros and duffers before they ever swing a club is the difference in the pace with which they play shots out of trouble. Pros and scratch golfers know that this shot is critical and consider all their options carefully before hitting the shot. Duffers, in contrast, speed through the shot at warp speed. Perhaps we are embarrassed to be in such dire straits. Being in the woods brands us as the truly awful golfers we are who don't deserve to be on the course. Never mind that even the best players hit into trouble; we know that this is not where we're supposed to hit the golf ball, and we want to get out of this situation as soon as possible. Worse than being embarrassed, we are just plain mad, and we plan to stay mad until we rectify this situation and get back into play like we should have been to begin with.

Observe your next round and notice how quickly you tend to play from trouble. With lightning speed a shot decision is made, a club is pulled from the bag, and with a quick practice swing, the ball goes careening off the nearest sapling, and we're still in trouble. On certain particularly entertaining occasions, this comedy of errors can reach a critical mass, producing a chain reaction of "Frankly, my dear, I don't give a damn" shots executed at breakneck speed.

Many blow-up holes are produced by rushing to get out of trouble. You need to take the time to calm down from the last shot and prepare to get out of trouble with the next shot. *Take your time.* Even if you took a few minutes to find your ball, this is not the time to pick up your pace of play. This is the time to think through your options, examine your lie, and make a good recovery shot. Whenever you are in trouble, take twice as long to prepare for and think through the shot as you would if you were in the fairway.

The primary focus when you are in trouble should be on getting back into the fairway. Take your stroke and be happy if it is only one stroke that you lost. Trying to make it up with some miraculous saving shot will almost always make things worse. The first thing you want to do is determine your options and consider each shot that is possible, including going out the same way your ball came into trouble. Then prioritize these possibilities—not based on how much closer to the hole you'll be, but on how likely it is that you can pull off the shot. Remember that duffers often overestimate their skills in this situation, so be conservative. Consider the lie of the ball, the freedom you have to swing the club, the space available for error. All these factors will influence the chance of pulling off the shot.

The next step is to determine if the likely outcome of the shot will (a) put you on the green, (b) give you an approach shot to the green, or (c) get you out of trouble, but without a true approach to the green. Unless the least risky shot is the one that also puts you on the green, then you want to choose the lowest risk shot that gives you an approach on the next shot. You know that you have a wide range of distance for which you are capable of landing the ball on the green. This is not the time to take a riskier path out of trouble just to be twenty yards closer to the hole. Your primary goal is to get out of trouble and give yourself a shot to the green. Only under the best of circumstances should you try to get to the green from a tee shot that is in trouble.

To improve your mental approach to the shot out of trouble, it helps to focus on the challenge before you rather than feeling sorry for yourself for being there in the first place. Think about the shot as if you and your playing partners were betting on who can make the best score on the hole from this spot. Would you be willing to wager that you could make a par or bogey from this spot? If you think you have a reasonable chance of making par from the trouble you are in, pick a strategy that will give you the best chance of saving par. Keep in mind that from trouble, you don't need to get the ball on the green to make par. A shot from trouble that gives you a good approach shot to the green still gives you a chance to one putt for a par. Grinding out from trouble and saving a bogey or par is one of the more satisfying parts of the game. View trouble as one of the great challenges of golf, and you'll find you perform much better in these situations.

Take it to the course

1. When in trouble, don't rush out of it. Take your time to plan your next shot.
2. Consider the possible ways out of trouble and select the one that has the best chance of giving you an approach shot, not the one that gets you closest to the green.
3. Shots from trouble are one of golf's greatest challenges. Relish the opportunity to save par or bogey from trouble.

Chapter 9

Approach Shot Strategy

Whether from a good tee shot or from a good recovery shot, you are now in position to go for the green. *Where's the pin?* and *Is the pin up or back?* is pretty much the extent of strategic thinking most recreational golfers engage in on the approach shot. There's clearly more strategy involved than this, and getting on or near the green on the approach shot gives you a shot at birdie and often ensures you no worse than a bogey.

Selecting the approach shot target

For most recreational golfers, where to hit the approach shot is a no-brainer—at the flag. Why would you hit it anywhere else? Of course, not even the pros fire at the pin on some holes. For the typical recreational golfer, the range of error on an approach shot is twenty to thirty yards in any direction from the pin. There is a lot of potential trouble within twenty to thirty yards of the pin. Think about it for a minute. What is the goal of your approach shot? Are you really good enough to give yourself a three-foot birdie putt? I know you've done it before, but even blind squirrels find a nut every once in a while. The approach goal of every recreational golfer should be to give ourselves a putt—preferably a makeable putt—but any putt will do.

Actually, our expectation of greens in regulation (GIR) for a round is too high. Pros average less than 12 of 18 GIR; the typical recreational golfer hits 4 to 6 GIR in a round. That's less than a third of greens that you should expect to hit in regulation. If you are a true duffer, anything in the vicinity of the green that gives you a chip shot is a reasonable goal. Given these more realistic expectations for your approach shot, anything around the green is reasonable, and the position of the pin on the green has absolutely nothing to do with the target of your approach shot.

On approach shots, try thinking like a golf architect. If the hole is well-designed, the architect has given you at least one dangerous approach and one safe approach. If water is on the right front, then the left front or back usually has room to bail out. If there is a large bunker guarding the front left, then there is usually room around the green on the right. Except when designed by the most devilish of architects (e.g., think Pete Dye), most holes have a designed safe shot opposite the danger. This is the area where you want to focus.

Based on the trouble you observe around the green, first decide on the safe side of the green. Some dangers are obvious, such as ponds and creeks, or bunkers that guard one section of the green. Other trouble is more subtle. One of the worst places for your approach shot is off the green closest to the hole, especially if the green is running away from you. There is no way you will get your chip within twenty feet of the hole from this location. Greenskeepers love to cut holes near the edge of the green. Even with no apparent trouble, shooting at these pin placements is sheer folly. If you miss the green on the short side, you can probably kiss your par goodbye. Decide the safer side of the green and pick a target near the center of the green that favors the safer side.

Having decided the safer side, now decide the safer distance. Let's suppose that there is a pond on the front right side of the green. If the architect is being kind, then there should be a nice open expanse of green and chipping area on the back left. In this situation, you have both distance and direction on your side to land in the safe area and miss the hazard. If the architect wants to be little crueler—and most of them do—then this opposite quadrant has its own share of trouble, and the only safe area is set up front left, on the opposite side from the pond but the same distance. Golf architects know that distance is easier to control than direction for most recreational golfers, so if a difficult hole has a bailout area, it is often positioned the same distance as the hazard, but on the opposite side of the green. Don't get suckered into a bad shot by this type of design. If danger is short, hit it long. If danger is long, hit it short. Use distance control *and* a target toward the safer side of the green to avoid trouble and put yourself on or around the green.

Before you ever pull a club from the bag, you want to:

1. Decide where the trouble is around the green.
2. Pick a target near the center of the green favoring the safer side.
3. Decide if the safer distance is long or short of the green and rely on distance more than direction to keep you out of trouble.

Before moving on to club selection on the approach shot, a word about the appropriate order for determining the approach shot strategy. Often, the last strategic thought of the recreational golfer on an approach shot is something like "make sure you don't hit it left into the water." So the last thought before hitting the shot is a bit like thinking "don't think about pink elephants." Telling yourself not to do something makes it more likely to happen. If your last thought is not to put the shot in the water on the left, then guess what you are most likely to do? You'll notice that the first step above is to determine where the trouble is, then the remainder of the steps focus on where you want to hit the shot, not where you don't want to hit it. Once you've identified the trouble around the green and decided on a safe target area, focus on that target and trust your target and distance.

Club selection

Distance control is the friend of the duffer on an approach shot. If you're a recreational golfer, it's anyone's guess what direction you'll hit an approach shot. I've played with golf partners for whom I'm not even 100 percent sure that I won't be hit if I stand beside them. As bad as our direction can be, we can usually control if we hit it 130 or 150 yards in these random directions as long as we hit the ball solid. Distance control, however, is much more than picking the club you hit that distance. These are the additional factors you need to consider:

1. Elevation to the green. You will need to go up a club if the green is elevated, maybe even two clubs if the hill is severe. Conversely, you will need to go down one or two clubs if the green is below where you are.

2. Wind. Most golfers consider the wind, but usually not enough. A breeze in your face is worth one club, but a wind strong enough that you can hear it going past you is easily worth two clubs. If you are unfortunate enough to be playing in small craft advisory conditions, then you need to think about three or more clubs up. The same cannot be said for hitting downwind. Because your ball is going in the same direction as the wind, it is not helped as much going downwind as it is hindered traveling upwind. When the downwind is strong enough to hear it blowing past you, then go down one club; otherwise, you can probably get by playing the same club you'd normally play from that distance.

3. Slope of the lie. If you are on an uphill lie, you will need to go up one club because the slope will put additional loft on the club. If you are on a downhill lie, you can go down one club, although the more critical issue in this situation is making you sure that your shoulders are parallel to the slope and that you hit down on the ball so you don't hit it thin. If you blade it, it doesn't matter what the loft of the club is.

As you can see, by the time you have taken all these factors into account, you could easily be hitting a four iron from 140 yards out.

You may have noticed the absence of the lie itself in determining distance. Although pros and low handicappers will hit "flyers" from the rough, most duffers hit flyers from every lie. When was the last time you had a ball backspin on a green? Any additional distance from the rough due to less backspin and more roll is more than offset by the slower swing speed going through the grass. Therefore, mid to high handicappers can usually leave the lie out of the distance equation. When lie does come into consideration, it is usually because the lie doesn't allow you get the clubface cleanly on the ball. In that case, it probably makes more sense to abandon the approach shot and just get back into the fairway.

Distance control is your friend. Decide if you are safer near the back or the front of the green. Adjust for elevation, wind, and slope, and then select the club that has the best chance of going that distance. If you've decided that shorter is safer, then give yourself the miss of not making it to the green. If you've decided that longer is safer, then allow yourself to hit it over the green if necessary.

Take it to the course

1. Locate the trouble around the green, including the short side of the green.
2. Pick a directional target near the center of the green that favors the safe side.
3. Select a distance opposite the trouble (hit long if trouble is short, hit short if trouble is long).
4. Consider elevation, wind, and slope in deciding club selection.
5. Focus on your target, not on the pin or on the danger around the green.

Chapter 10

Around the Green Shot Strategy

Duffers probably waste more strokes around the green than any-where else. This is the area where pars quickly become snow-men as you chip back and forth across the green or chili dip your chip shot. Since duffers seldom hit the green in regulation, there is an increased demand to have a solid short game strategy around the green to minimize the risk of wasting strokes. Unfortunately, on and around the green is where most duffers relax and lose focus and aggressiveness. Perhaps we are so pleased that we accomplished get-ting on or near the green that we let down our focus and assume we'll two putt or get up and down, but this is the time to increase focus and be aggressive shot makers.

From around the green, the goal for any duffer should be to put the ball anywhere on the green. Although it would be nice to get up and down from around the green, you want to make sure above all else that your next shot is a putt. Keeping this goal in mind will lead you to make very different decisions around the green. It is not necessary to aim at the flag. If there is a bunker between you and the flag, but a shot twenty feet right of the pin takes the bunker out of play, take it. There also is no need for the perfect finesse shot that flies the bunker and stops next to a pin tucked just over the bunker. Make sure you clear the bunker, rough, or any other obstacle between you and the green, even if it goes thirty feet past the pin.

The typical mid to high handicapper is an interesting animal around the greens. Even though they seldom—if ever—practice their short game, they expect that they can manufacture a wide array of shots that would make any professional proud. Get your head out of the clouds and keep the game simple. You probably have one short pitch shot that you are comfortable with—use it. You probably have only one sand shot that you can consistently get out of the bunker with most of the time—use it. You probably have one chip shot that you can execute—use it. This is where reading golf instruction books and magazines will kill your game. Unless you have practiced these variations, you don't need to worry about altering swing paths, ball position in your stance, or varying the loft of the clubface. If you have only one sand shot swing that you have practiced, then that is the swing you should always use in the sand, even if it puts the ball thirty feet short or long of the pin. Once you've mastered one type of chip, pitch, or sand shot, then maybe you can practice a different type of short shot, but the golf course is not the time to try out new shots you've never attempted before.

As with the approach shot, it is important to consider the greatest area of trouble and the safest area where you want to put your shot. For most golfers, the greatest trouble around the green is often right in front of them. If you are in the rough or in a bunker, you want to make sure, first and foremost, that you get out of the rough or bunker. The fat chip or pitch leaves you in the same mess you are presently in, so it's critical to think *ball first* and *accelerate* on any shot around the green. Most duffers would score better hitting every shot around the green thin versus fat. Give yourself permission to hit the ball well past the hole as long as you end up on the green, putting for your next shot.

Whenever possible, putt. Putt from the fringe, from a good lie in the rough, from ten feet off the green in the fairway, or from a trap without a significant lip. You know how to putt; you've done it plenty of times. And you are almost guaranteed of getting the ball closer to the pin than if you use an iron. The corollary of this rule is to prefer the lower path for any short shot. If you are deciding between a high pitch or a low chip, choose the low chip shot. You want to get the ball back on the ground and rolling to the pin as soon as you can.

Before the shot, picture an area about the size of a child's wading pool. This is the area you want to put the shot in. Anything in that area is a great shot that gives you a very makeable putt for par. As your handicap drops, the size of this area can decrease (e.g., Hula-Hoop, whiskey barrel), but all you are trying to do is give yourself a potentially makeable putt on the next shot.

Now that you have the target in mind, picture the shot that will get you there. Again, pick the shot that will get the ball on the ground the soonest and roll to the target. Picture how far you want the ball to fly, where you want it to land (another wading pool area), and where you want it to end up. If the picture of that shot looks funny to you, then it's probably the wrong shot. Visualize different flights and rolls until you have something in your mind that looks reasonable, then choose the club and type of shot (from the few that you are comfortable executing) that will come the closest to what you picture.

Notice that this is the first place that visualization has come into the discussion. With most tee shots and approach shots, visualization has little value for the typical recreational golfer. Visualization is not magic. When you visualize a shot, your brain automatically rehearses the complex series of actions and feelings that it has learned through producing that shot multiple times. If you've seldom produced the shot being visualized, your brain doesn't have enough information to rehearse the shot you have in mind. So why visualize shots around the green? Although the more you practice your short game, the better that visualization will work, you've probably hit your standard chip, pitch, or sand shot enough times in the past for your brain to have some idea of how this shot should be executed. More importantly, chips, pitches, and sand shots are finesse shots that require considerable feel. Visualization replaces the mechanical thoughts that freeze you up with a more intuitive feeling for the shot you need to execute. Picture what you want the ball to do and trust your brain to piece together the swing that will produce that shot based on your past experience hitting that shot.

For most duffers, the short game around the green is where the most strokes can be made up. It is what separates pars and bogeys from doubles, triples, and more. Take your time preparing for this shot and thinking through the options available to you. Once you've decided your strategy for the shot, visualize the shot and put a confident stroke on the ball. Recreational golfers tend to have a split personality on shots around the green. Initially, they believe they can hit an amazing shot that most pros wouldn't attempt, but then when they are over the ball, doubt sets in, and they put a tentative stroke on the ball. You need to reverse this mindset. Plan a conservative shot that maximizes your chances of ending up on the green, and then play that shot confidently and aggressively.

Take it to the course

1. Around the green, consider your options and plan a shot that will get you on the green, even if not near the hole.
2. Rely on trusted, practiced chips, pitches, and sand strokes; the round is not the time to manufacture a shot you've never performed before.
3. Visualize the shot you want to hit and rely on intuitive feel more than swing mechanics.
4. Plan a conservative shot around the green, but execute it aggressively and confidently.

Chapter 11

Strategy on the Green

Putting doesn't require much strategy. See the hole—putt it there. There are, however, a few strategic thoughts on the green that will help your game and reduce the number of three putts. First, you need to have a sense for the length of your "sure," "makeable," and "lag" putts. For most golfers, the sure putt is within one pace or so (within two to four feet). It is the distance where you expect to sink nearly all your putts. The makeable putt is usually within about six or seven paces (within around twenty feet) and is the length where you have at least some reasonable chance of making the putt. Outside of this range is your lag putt range. You intuitively know these distances: a sure putt is one you expect to almost always make, a makeable putt is one in which you hope you can make and wouldn't be surprised if it went in, and a lag putt is a putt that you would be quite surprised if it went in.

For anything in your lag putt range, you are not even concerned about the hole; you want to leave your ball in the best position for the next putt. Direction is of little to no concern; all you want to worry about is speed and distance. Since most golfers prefer an uphill putt with a minimal break for their sure putt, this is the position you want to leave yourself after a lag putt if possible. Picture a Hula-Hoop area around the hole and putt at a speed that will leave you inside this area. Again, distance is your only real concern, not direction. We've all played with people who, over a forty-foot putt, incessantly line up the putt and plumb their putter to determine the break. Who are they kidding? Unless the break is severe, the ball is moving too fast during most of the putt for the break to affect the line much. Missing that Hula-Hoop-sized area is seldom a problem of putting on the correct line; it is a problem of putting at the right speed. Worrying about the line and focusing on the hole only serves to tense you up, causing you to lose the feel that you desperately need on lag putts. Picture a Hula-Hoop and just hit the ball hard enough to get inside that Hula-Hoop.

For makeable putts, the strategy is a bit different. Distance and direction carry equal weight on these putts. This is where you can gain or lose a number of strokes. You want to be the most focused and the most aggressive that you can be over these putts. Read the break, determine the line, and then determine the speed with the goal of putting the ball a foot or two past the hole if it misses. Most of the time, duffers hit these makeable putts short. "Never up, never in" is particularly applicable for these makeable putts within twenty feet. You want to focus on making this putt, not on the bad things that will happen if you miss. Don't be tentative. Be aggressive and go for the hole.

For sure putts, direction is your primary focus, and speed should be of only secondary concern. Unfortunately, some golfers make speed an issue by being tentative over these sure putts and coming up short, or decelerating and pushing or pulling the putt. Again, you want to be firm with this putt so it will go a foot or two past the hole if you miss it. There is no reason for the ball to limp into the front edge of the hole. Pick a spot on the backside of the cup and focus on hitting this spot with your putt. Being firm and aggressive over these putts also allows you to take most of the break out of the putt. Except for the most severe breaks, you don't want to give the hole away. Pick your line and make a firm, aggressive putt into the hole. Ben Crenshaw could drop the putt into the front edge of the hole, but he had exceptional putting feel, even for a pro. Duffers don't have that kind of feel, so our best strategy is to putt it into the back of the cup.

Reading breaks. You've probably heard that amateur golfers tend to underread the break of a putt, missing the putt on the low side of the hole. Part of the problem is underreading the break. There is a crescent of possible lines from the ball to the hole, and recreational golfers tend to take the low road most of the time. But the other problem is speed. With enough speed, the low line would have a chance of going in. It may run five feet past the hole if missed, but it has a chance of going in. Usually, the putt misses below the hole on a break because the duffer doesn't read enough break *and* doesn't stroke the putt firmly enough. You want to find a line in the middle of the crescent—maybe even slightly to the high side of the middle—and putt the ball with enough speed to run past the hole by a foot or two if you miss it.

If you have difficulty reading breaks, think like the golf architect. The architect has to design a green so water doesn't puddle on it but runs off instead. Ask yourself where the water runs off the green, especially the direction it runs off near the hole. Your putt is slowest around the hole and will break the most near the hole, so the break near the hole should be your primary concern. For this reason, it is often helpful, particularly on longer putts, to read the break from the hole and from a point on the line of the putt closer to the hole.

Don't overread breaks. Pros play on lightning-fast greens that accentuate breaks. Recreational golfers play on slow greens that get too much traffic to be cut short. This is another reason duffers should save their aggressiveness for the green. The greens we putt on are slower than usual and break less than usual, allowing us to put a confident and aggressive stroke on the ball.

Visualizing the line. As should be clear by now, I think that visualization is highly overrated for the typical recreational golfer. Visualization allows your brain to rehearse the complex orchestration of inputs and outputs that have produced the shot that you visualize, but this is only possible if you have hit the shot you are visualizing enough times with enough consistency to give your brain a clue of what it should be rehearsing. That's why when you visualize hitting a high draw on your drive, you usually picture it from the third person, as if watching someone on TV hit the shot. Your brain hasn't seen the shot enough from you to picture it from the first-person perspective.

Although visualization isn't particularly useful for recreational golfers on their wood and iron shots, it is potentially useful on pitch and chip shots and is especially useful for putts. In contrast to drives, putting is a relatively simple set of movements. If you don't believe me, just think about those two-year-olds on the miniature golf course who can solidly putt the ball in the general direction of the hole, but you wouldn't expect that same two-year-old to hit a ball with a driver on the practice range. The combination of a simpler set of movements, increased need for feel, and the fact that you have numerous experiences with putting makeable distances and breaks makes visualization a useful strategy when you are putting.

Visualize the putt from behind or beside the ball. You want your brain to see the putt from the same perspective it has seen similar putts before. You may want to determine the break from a number of positions including behind the ball, behind the hole, and from the low side of the putt, but after you have determined the break, you want to visualize the putt from behind the ball. Picture the entire journey of the ball from the time it leaves your putter until it drops into the cup. Done well, your visualization should produce an image of a highlighted track on the green that your ball will roll on as it makes its way to the hole. Pick a spot on this track that is within your peripheral vision as you stand over the ball, usually within a few inches of the ball, to use as an alignment aid. Use the mental image of the track you've pictured in your mind to feel the speed of the putt.

With the mental image of the track from your putter to the hole and the alignment spot that sets the initial direction of the putt, you shouldn't even need to look at the hole to make the putt. Your brain has everything it needs to make the putt. Nearly everyone is uncomfortable standing over the putt without looking at the hole again, but you may want to practice putting without looking at the hole anymore once you've set the line and have the putt visualized well enough that you can see it in your mind. You might be surprised how well you putt. Once you've taken your stance, it doesn't hurt to look at the hole again to see the path of the ball one last time before you putt, but whatever you do, don't adjust your alignment or change your visualization of the putt based on this last look. If you see something you didn't see before, step back and go through your pre-putt routine again.

There is research that encourages recreational golfers to look at the hole the entire time they putt, not at the ball. Of course, I've seldom seen anyone using this strategy on the course because it is so different from everything else we do. On every other golf stroke, we look at the ball, not where we want it to go. Hockey players look at the puck, not the net. When I sweep the walkway or rake the leaves in my yard, I look where I'm sweeping or raking, not where what I'm sweeping or raking will go. So even if some research shows that you may putt better if you look at the hole, it just seems to be more familiar to look at the object we want to make contact with. However, one reason the "look at the hole" strategy may be helpful is because it reinforces your visualization of the putt and forces you to trust that your brain and body will produce the putt you have visualized. The same process is possible if, while looking at the ball, you visualize the putt in your mind. As you stroke the putt, your mind should focus on the path of the ball as you have visualized it.

The short putt mental game

You've probably noticed the difference in tension and anxiety that you feel over a birdie versus double-bogey putt or a sure putt versus a makeable putt. Rationally, all putts count the same on your scorecard, but our mind makes some putts more important than others. We tend to be more nervous and tentative over a par putt of three feet versus twenty feet. Why? Even a two-year-old can make a three-foot putt, and that's the problem. Everyone expects us to make the three-footer whereas nobody expects us to make the twenty-footer. If we make the twenty-footer, we are steely-eyed putting aces, but if we miss the three-footer, we are chokers who can't make a putt when it matters. And if it's a three-footer for a birdie, we become nearly paralyzed in fear.

Recreational golfers have come up with a few ways to cope with this short putt anxiety, but most of them are maladaptive. One strategy is to become more deliberate and cautious about the putt, particularly if it's for birdie or par. But the longer you take over a putt, the more time you give yourself to think about its importance and let the tension build. In addition, altering your normal putting routine produces more nervousness, not less.

The opposite strategy is to quickly putt and "get it over with." This tactic is an attempt to avoid the anxiety by rushing the putt. It is most commonly seen when "finishing up" after lagging a putt within a few feet. Instead of marking the ball and waiting until you are up again, you quickly walk to where the lag putt ended, rush the preshot routine, and make a hurried stroke on the ball. This may make you less anxious, but the outcome is still bad.

A corollary fear-avoidance strategy is the cavalier, nonchalant putt. I must admit that this has been one of my many golf weaknesses. I've lagged a putt outside the gimme range, but treat it as if one of my partners has given me the putt, quickly walk up to it, and one-hand it toward the hole. And if I miss it, I'm ashamed to admit that I've sometimes scored it as if it were a gimme. I know, the USGA should revoke my membership. What a perversion of the rules of golf—all because I can't handle the anxiety of making or missing a short putt. Needless to say, my priority for improving how I play golf is to make a real stroke on even the shortest of putts and to count every putt.

This brings me to a diversion about "gimmes." When I was learning the game, I played mostly on busy public courses, and my dad didn't want us to hold up play. As a result, I learned to play at a good pace, but I also learned to take gimmes. It does speed up the game a little, but also produces considerable anxiety about making short putts. Over time, short putts become foreign to us because we haven't putted them; they've been given to us. Every recreational golfer should vow to make every putt—no gimmes. Not only is it in the spirit of the rules of golf, but it will make us stronger and more confident when we really need to make a short putt.

So what should you do over short putts to reduce the tension? First, remind yourself that every putt counts the same, whether it's a two-foot birdie putt or a twenty-foot double bogey putt. Second, take a deep breath (from the diaphragm) and visualize the putt just as do for every putt. Third, treat the short putt the same as any putt. Line up the putt as you would any putt. Go through the same preshot routine as you would for any putt. And finally, be aggressive. It is amazing that the same duffer who aggressively drives the ball from the tee and risks considerable trouble by doing so will subsequently take a tentative, fearful short putt. Putt aggressively with confidence, especially when making a "sure" putt.

Take it to the course

1. Know whether you are putting a "sure," "makeable," or "lag" putt.
2. On lag putts, focus primarily on speed and on getting the ball into the "sure" putt area.
3. On makeable putts, be aggressive and balance speed and direction.
4. Treat sure putts the same as you do all putts; don't overanalyze or rush these putts.
5. Read the break from various perspectives and consider how water drains off the green, particularly near the hole.
6. Visualize the path of the putt from the putter to the cup.
7. Let your body use the image of the putt to put a solid, confident stroke on the ball.

Chapter 12

Preshot Routine

If you haven't noticed yet, one of the major themes of this book is that making good transitions is critical for all golfers, particularly recreational golfers. Duffers have to make good transitions from the drudgery of our hectic lives to playing the game we love, putting our daily worries behind us to focus on golf. Duffers also have many more opportunities than the pros to make good transitions from a bad shot to a good shot. The most important transition, however, is from not making a stroke to making a stroke. In between shots, we curse past shots, make fun of our partners' shots, ride around in the golf cart, drink beer, and tell lies about our golf game. At some point after this frivolity between shots, we need to focus on the next shot. This transition from not hitting the ball to hitting the ball is the essence of the preshot routine. Unfortunately, most duffers don't have one, or at least don't have a good one. Having watched my share of mediocre to bad golfers, many lack of a consistent preshot routine. They may think they have a preshot routine, but they usually don't. Here are some examples of bad preshot routines.

Practice till perfect. This is an interesting routine. The golfer takes practice swing after practice swing next to the ball until they "feel" the right swing. If the practice swing results in hitting the ground too hard or missing the ground entirely, they do it again. If their balance was not right or the club slipped in their hands, they do it again. When the "good" practice swing has been practiced (usually after three or four swings) they then slide up to the ball and swing. Of course, they left the only good swing they had in the practice sequence, and the doubt produced from multiple bad swings before stumbling on a good one ensures that the actual swing will not be very good.

Set up rigor mortis. Have you ever wondered if the person you are playing with has had some sort of stroke or petite mal seizure while addressing the ball? I've never understood this preshot routine. First, very little happens before addressing the ball. Then, once over the ball, the golfer falls into some sort of trance or suspended animation. I assume they are waiting for some sort of divine inspiration that now is the time to begin the backswing, but it must never come given the outcome of the shot. Actually, most golfers who stand over the ball too long are usually rehearsing a litany of swing thoughts and/or waiting for their anxiety to decrease enough to feel comfortable about the shot. It never happens.

Rituals to the golf gods. Although a consistent routine reduces anxiety, these golfers have taken it to a new level. Rituals or compulsions often develop to prevent negative events that are frequently out of our control, so the golf shot, especially for the duffer, is a prime situation for ritualistic behavior. These golfers have an elaborate procedure in which each step of the routine is tightly scripted and cannot be altered in any way. Clubs, towels, tees, and balls all must be handled a certain way in a certain sequence to produce a good shot. Of course, any distraction or disruption during this ritual causes the golfer to restart the ritual from scratch. Although this may reduce their anxiety about the shot if they can perform it, the ritual has grown into such an uncontrollable monster that the focus is more on the ritual itself than on the golf shot.

Try them all out. These are the golfers who have watched too many preshot routines on TV. For each round and often multiple times during the round, they morph into one of their favorite pro golfers, attempting to mimic his or her preshot routine. If it works for a pro, it must work for me. Of course, when that routine doesn't work, they try another routine. They don't get that it is not the substance of the routine, but the consistency of the routine that's important.

Grip it and rip it. This is the "anti preshot routine" routine. For these golfers, nothing seems to work to make them comfortable and ready to swing, so what the hell, just walk up to the ball and hit it. This is similar to not studying for a test so you don't feel as bad when you fail it. If you thought about it, you would feel uncomfortable with what you are about to do, so don't think about it. Although this bypasses the preshot nerves, it also leads to being ill-prepared to execute the shot.

Developing a consistent preshot routine

So what is a reasonable preshot routine? The preshot routine should do two things for you; it should get you prepared and focused to hit a good shot, and it should be routine enough that you are comfortable about the shot and focused on the shot, not on your preshot routine. What you do and how long it takes to do it are not as important as doing it consistently. What follows are recommendations about what should be occurring during your preshot routine, but you need to find your own content and sequence for your preshot routine, one that you can feel comfortable with and do consistently without thinking about it.

Before we discuss what is in a preshot routine, it is important to remember what is not in it. First, there is no continued thinking about what shot to play. The strategy about what shot to play should occur before you put a club in your hand. If you are in your preshot routine and have competing thoughts about how or where to play the shot, then you need to step back and start again. Before you start the preshot routine, you should have committed to the strategy and the shot you are about to hit.

Second, there should be as little instructional thought as possible about your swing. If you have a swing key or two that you want to rehearse in the practice swing, that's fine. What you don't want to do is go through a checklist of proper swing mechanics on every shot.

The preshot routine is designed to clear your mind and focus you on the shot to be executed.

So if you're not supposed to think, what do you do in the preshot routine?

1. Visualize what you expect the shot to do. I realize that I've made a big deal thus far that visualization is less useful for duffers, particularly for drives and approach shots. That said, visualization of a shot you've hit numerous times in the past is usually helpful, but should be a realistic picture, not nirvana. If you usually hit a low slice off the tee, there is no sense in visualizing a high draw. Instead, picture that low slice that you've hit numerous times from the moment it leaves your club until it lands.

2. While visualizing the shot, take a slow or mini practice swing. You want to match the image of the shot with the feeling that is associated with that image. If you need a swing thought or two to help you do this, that's fine, but you want to keep this from being an internal coaching session. The idea is to picture the shot and let your body simply practice producing it.

3. Lock in the line. If you watch pro golfers, this is when they get serious and focused during their preshot routine. After visualizing the shot and taking a couple of small practice swings, they focus intensely on the line they want to swing on. Draw a mental line from a few feet behind the ball to the target. Pick a spot on the ground a few feet from your ball to help you lock in the line.

4. Set up for the shot. Take your stance and grip in whatever way is comfortable for you, so you are set up on the line you have chosen. Stance and grip are two things that you can make sure are right before you begin the swing sequence, so feel free to go through a grip and stance checklist to put yourself in position to make a good swing, but keep the checklist short. More than two or three steps in the stance and grip sequence will produce tension and divert

your focus from the goal of hitting the ball where you want to hit it. A consistent setup routine ensures that the fundamentals are in place for a good shot.

5. Waggle. Before beginning the swing, most golfers have a small movement of the club that helps them relax and get comfortable over the ball. Some people do a mini-rehearsal of the takeaway. Others lift the club above the ball and simulate the wrist release at impact. Still, others press their grip or press their hands forward before starting the swing. What you do is not as important as doing something consistently. You want to develop a simple movement prior to the swing that reduces muscle tension and triggers your brain and body to execute the swing.

You'll notice that there is no recommendation of a full practice swing next to the ball during your preshot routine. Getting rid of this part of the preshot ritual, or at least reducing it to only one full practice swing, can be difficult but is likely to improve your shots. The reasons for dropping the full-speed practice swing by the ball are simple. First, these practice swings next to the ball typically put more tension and doubt into your swing, not less. How many times has a less than stellar practice swing made you worry about what would happen on the actual shot? For most duffers, the practice swing produces more doubt than confidence in the actual shot. Second, it is likely that during these full-speed practice swings, you have moved your grip or posture or stance. Therefore, if you feel you need a full practice swing, then don't just slide up the ball and hit it. Instead, be sure to restart the grip and stance routine prior to the actual shot to be sure you are set up correctly. Third, you want a clear transition in your preshot routine between getting ready to swing and actually getting down to the business of swinging. There should be a point before every swing when you tune out the outside world and any internal running commentary and focus solely on executing the shot. The most common place to make that transition is after you have lined up the shot and are stepping up to the ball. From that point onward, you want to be about the business of hitting the ball, not practicing to do it.

The only reasonable exception to eliminating the practice stroke next to the ball may be in the short game. Although all the above reasons apply for taking your practice chips or putts behind the ball as well, it is often difficult for a golfer to get a good sense of the speed of the clubhead they want to produce for a finesse shot without standing next to the ball to do so. Therefore, for chips, pitches, and putts, you may want to build in a practice stroke or two next to the ball. However, it is still critical that you make a clean shift to the task of chipping or putting. Some golfers do this by stepping away one last time before getting over the putt or chip to execute it. Others take a final look at the line of the putt or chip, then focus back on the ball to make the transition. Whatever you do, make sure that you feel that you make a clearly defined shift from practicing to performing.

Remember that nothing in the rules says that you have to take a practice chip, pitch, or putting stroke before you do it for real. You do lots of other fine motor tasks without a practice stroke first. You don't take practice pitches in slow-pitch softball, or practice dart throws before throwing darts. In most other feel or finesse sports movements, there is no practice of the movement just before it is executed. Instead, we mentally see what we want to do and let our minds produce the body feel we need to execute these fine motor actions. I know it's difficult to give up a ritual like the practice putt or chip or pitch, and a practice stroke may be something you feel you need to execute a stroke, but the next time you find yourself struggling with your short game and putting, try stroking the ball without a practice stroke.

Take it to the course

1. Develop a consistent preshot routine that you use for every shot.
2. After determining your strategy for the shot, use your preshot routine to shift your focus to the shot at hand and to feel comfortable over the ball.
3. Consider dropping the full practice swings next to the ball. Instead, when you are ready to hit the shot, step up to it and hit it.

Chapter 13

The Glory of Grinding

We all have fond memories of great golf rounds. Days when we could do no wrong; every shot was solid and putts rolled in like magic. These are the rounds that keep us coming back, even if they are quite infrequent. But it is also important to find glory in grinding out a round.

Even pros have wide variability in how well they play each round. On the same course with similar conditions, they can shoot 67 one day and 77 the next. Duffers have even larger variability in how well we play. Within a few weeks on the same course, I can score in the low 80s or the high 90s.

It is important not only to accept this variability but embrace it. Within a few holes, we can usually determine if we have our A game or our F game. One option if we're having a bad day is to simply give up mentally—not care anymore about our score and focus instead on drinking beer the rest of the round. There is an alternative—to find joy in grinding out a bad round.

I have found golf to be one of the more character-building activities, and that character building has often come from having to work through a round when I'm not playing well. After a few holes, it is clear that something is wrong with my swing, that I can't fix it during the round, and that if I am going to stay engaged in the round, I will need to grind out a respectable round. I realize that I'm going to have to face a number of challenging shots—through trees, out of tall rough, out of bunkers—because I put myself in these challenging situations.

It Is easy to give up under these circumstances. We came to play golf to have fun, not to grind out a bad round. It's not the same as breaking 80, but there is satisfaction in shooting 95 by grinding out a bad round that could easily have been 105. From every bad spot on the course that you put yourself in, accept the challenge of if and how you can get from this spot to making a par or a bogey, or even a double or triple bogey. Each hole becomes its own challenge. This is not the time for heroic rescue shots; it is a time to take safe, high probability rescue shots. This is not the round to think about hitting the green in regulation but instead just getting somewhere in the general proximity of the green. And it is not the round to expect to make long putts, but just to minimize three putt greens.

You'll have bad rounds—everyone does—but if you embrace grinding out a reasonable score while playing badly, it improves your mental game and gives you more practice at rescue shots. You may even find you feel some satisfaction from a score that is far from great but could have been much worse.

Take it to the course

1. Recognize that there is a wide range of the game you take to the course and that you'll sometimes play badly.
2. Instead of giving up after a few holes, challenge yourself to grind out the best score you can despite not having your A-game this round.
3. Take each shot out of trouble as a challenge to make the best score you can, even if the best score possible from that trouble is a double or triple bogey.
4. Find satisfaction in scoring better than you could have given how badly you were striking the ball during the round.

Chapter 14

Taking Care of Yourself During the Round

Let's face it, golf is not the Ironman Triathlon. Played with a cart, the sport is no more physically grueling than walking the dog. A round in which you walk and carry your bag, however, provides a sustained moderate-intensity physical workout. Taking care of yourself physically during a round of golf is important not only for your physical state, but also for your mental state. Our brains use considerable energy to operate efficiently. Dehydration and inadequate energy intake take their toll on the brain's ability to focus, concentrate, and assess the probabilities of various shot options. Being "too tired to think" results in poor golf decisions, particularly in the later part of the round when these decisions are crucial to shooting a good score. By keeping your brain and body in good shape during the round, you can maintain your ability to make good golf decisions throughout the round.

I realize that to be a card-carrying duffer, you have to treat your body badly on the course. Most golf packages include a complimentary breakfast where golfers load up on enough eggs and breakfast meats to clog every artery. Beer drinking begins after noon, which through a mystery of the time-space continuum actually begins around 9:00 a.m. on most golf courses. And to stay hydrated on the course, they call them "beer carts" for a reason. For food, these "beer carts" are well stocked with nutritious foods like candy bars and chips. And if that's not enough, people who would otherwise never smoke a cigarette feel the need to smoke a cigar on the course. Recreational golf is not as healthy a pursuit as some would like to think.

Despite this physical abuse, most duffers are genuinely surprised when they play badly. Who'd have thought you would have difficulty making that six-foot putt with a blood alcohol level that would get you tossed in jail if you were driving a car? Golf is as much an opportunity for camaraderie with friends as a game or sport. For some golfing partners, a round of golf serves the same purpose as going to a sports bar or pool hall. If that's why you're playing golf, then enjoy yourself, but adjust your golf score expectations accordingly.

If you want to score well, however, you need to take care of your brain and body during the round. I realize that taking care of yourself may be a foreign concept for most duffers, so here are a few tips:

1. Stay hydrated. You probably know that drinking water decreases the chance of muscle cramps, but it also decreases the chance of "brain cramps." The brain functions best when it is sufficiently hydrated. Be sure to drink plenty of water during the round, even if it is not hot. You should drink about half the daily amount of water needed on the course. That daily amount depends on your weight, but a good rule of thumb is half your body weight in ounces of water. Therefore, if you are two hundred pounds, you need to drink about one hundred ounces of water each day. If you drink half of that amount on the course, then that's fifty ounces or about four twelve-ounce bottles of water on the course. Yes, that comes to almost a half-gallon of water, but that is what your body and brain need to function well on the golf course.

2. Stay nourished. If you are on the course and it's been more than three or four hours since you last ate, make sure to eat a snack. Your muscles need fuel to burn, and most of the readily available fuel is gone after four hours. For most people, getting a light snack at the turn is adequate. Unfortunately, the typical fare of most clubhouse grills (hot dogs, potato chips, and candy bars) are not what your body needs. Choose pretzels, crackers, or nuts, preferably unsalted, if they are available since they will give you the slow-burning carbohydrates you need without a lot of what you don't need. Fruit is also a great choice, but not typically found at

most clubhouses. Given how much most clubhouses charge for a hot dog, you are better off financially as well as physically if you bring a piece of fruit and a bag of pretzels with you to the course.

3. Stay loose and warmed up. Especially when play is slow and you are waiting between shots, take the time to stretch. Golf is a game of brief bouts of muscle exertion followed by long periods of minimal activity, a situation ripe for muscle stiffness and injury. When waiting on the tee or in the fairway, take the opportunity to stretch, do some loose practice swings, or walk around a bit. Using these slow periods to stay loose and warmed up also gives you something to do instead of getting frustrated by the slow play.

In addition to staying hydrated, nourished, and loose during the round, there is one important thing to avoid when playing golf—drugs. You're probably wondering when cocaine abuse became a problem among golfers, but I'm referring to the legal drugs: caffeine, nicotine, and alcohol.

Caffeine: Caffeine is most often associated with coffee, but it is also found to a lesser degree in tea, soft drinks, and chocolate. And caffeine is available in much more concentrated dosages in various energy drinks. Caffeine is a mild stimulant that increases heart rate, restricts blood flow, and increases muscle tension. Coffee and tea are also diuretics that rob your body of fluids, something you particularly want to avoid in the summer heat. Caffeine is among the most benign of drugs, and, in moderation, has a number of positive effects on cognitive functioning.

So should you avoid caffeine while golfing? In moderation and consistent with your usual caffeine intake, coffee and other caffeine products won't hurt your mental game and may actually improve it slightly. But be careful not to overdue your caffeine consumption, and avoid the caffeine-laden energy drinks. Most duffers are tense enough and rush their golf shots enough already without adding a caffeine buzz. So don't abstain, but limit your coffee and caffeine consumption to the low end of what you usually drink.

Nicotine: Smoking was a regular part of golf until the 1970s when the serious health dangers of smoking became clear, and smoking gradually became socially unacceptable. Unfortunately, in recent years there has been a resurgence of golf course smoking in the form of cigars. Thousands of golfers who otherwise would not smoke feel the desire to light up a cigar on the course. Why? Some golfers believe that smoking a cigar relaxes them and improves their game. Others do it simply because a golf course is one of the few public places where it is acceptable to smoke a cigar. It may feel like you are relaxing when puffing on a cigar, but nicotine is a stimulant, so you will probably have a harder time staying relaxed during the round.

If you don't smoke, there's no need to smoke on the course. Avoid cigars and other tobacco products during the round. Tobacco products will not improve your performance and are usually just one more thing to contend with that breaks up your preshot routine. Even if you're a regular smoker, smoking as little as you need to keep the feeling of withdrawal at bay is preferable to smoking more than usual just because you are outside and can smoke as much as you want. Most importantly, if you want to be alive and healthy enough during retirement to play golf regularly, then seek assistance to quit smoking now.

Alcohol: I must admit that I think beer carts are among the major advances in recreational golf in the last century. Unfortunately, golf rounds are often ruined by drinking on the course.

Some golfers think that a beer relaxes them and improves their game. Alcohol is a depressant and does reduce muscle tension. If you have recently eaten and have some tolerance to alcohol, then a beer or two during a round may not hurt your game. Unfortunately, even at low doses, alcohol has significant effects on fine motor skills and eye-hand coordination. Who needs fine motor skills and eye-hand coordination to play golf anyway? Those beers at the turn taste really good, but when you are standing over a makeable par putt on 18 to break the score you've been trying to break for the last decade, you'll probably wish you had every ounce of eye-hand coordination and fine motor skills you can muster. Save the beer and other alcoholic beverages for celebrating after the round. If beer is an integral part of the golfing experience for you and your partners, then make sure you have eaten something, and drink slowly over the course of the round. Alternating water and beer is a good way to pace your alcohol consumption on the course.

The fact that these substances are part of the golf experience is further evidence that golf is not the most physically demanding of sports. You don't see marathoners puffing on a cigar or grabbing a beer as they run by the refreshment stations. Because the physical demands on a golfer—particularly the average cart-driving duffer—are not great, most golfers can consume these substances on the course without negatively impacting the physical aspects of the game. Even while smoking or with a few beers, you can still swing a club, get in the cart, drive to your ball, and get out to swing the club again. Golf, however, is one of the most mentally demanding sports, and the use of these substances, particularly alcohol, impairs mental functions that could be used to play better.

Taking care of yourself on the course primarily involves taking care of your mental state. Golf is a mentally taxing sport. For over four hours, you must shift numerous times from general inattention to intense, focused attention to each shot. You must stay calm and focused simultaneously. You must be able to maintain a focus on your game for a long period of time in a wide range of conditions and situations. Becoming a Zen master would probably be the best training for the mental endurance test that is golf. Unfortunately, most of us live with job stress, rush hours, family commitments, and the general pressure of life for most of our non-golf existence, and we look to golf as a retreat from our stressful lifestyle. Somehow, we are supposed to turn off our normal mental state that is far from conducive to the mental demands of golf and shift to a state of peaceful focus. Who says this game isn't hard?

Take it to the course

1. Stay hydrated on the course—with water.
2. Stay nourished on the course with fruits and complex carbohydrates like pretzels and crackers.
3. Limit caffeine and alcohol drinks on the course.
4. If you don't smoke, the golf course isn't the place to begin.
5. And if you decide that for this round you are more interested in having fun with your friends than playing well, then ignore points 1–4 above, but don't expect that you'll also score well.

Chapter 15

The Mental Game Is the Game

When I started playing golf, the game was all about ball striking. The joy of golf was found in long drives and accurate approach shots that had a perfect trajectory. I suspect many golfers think that this is all that golf is about. Certainly, that's the impression you get from your playing partners who "ooh" and "aah" when you crush a drive or put a little backspin on your approach shot, but don't seem to be as impressed when you recover from a bad shot.

The funny thing is that I would often complete a round feeling good about my ball striking, only to have my scorecard not reflect how I felt about the round. There are no style points in golf for hitting it long or hitting the ball on the perfect trajectory. Golf is not figure skating. There are no judges to rate your performance. All that matters is how few strokes it takes to get the ball in the hole.

Although it was many years ago, I still remember stringing together two excellent shots on a long, tight par four with water in front of the green. I was quite impressed with myself that I made the green in regulation on this difficult hole. I expected my playing partner to be duly impressed, but instead, he said, "Now you need to finish it." It occurred to me at that moment that I had already mentally checked out of the hole. I had hit two great shots and was on the green. What more was I to do? Of course, I then proceeded to three-putt the green and walk away with the same bogey I could have made by driving it short in the rough, laying up in front of the water, pitching onto the green, and two putting. The latter way doesn't get the "oohs" and "aahs" from your playing partners, but it results in the exact same score.

This realization led to a number of changes in how I played the game. First, I put much greater focus, both in practice and on the course, on my short game. At the practice range, I spent half of my time hitting chips and pitches. I would swing by the course after work just to spend time on the practice green before heading home. Most importantly, on the course, I realized that I needed to shift my attention and concentration more to what I did around and on the green. A serviceable drive and solid iron shot were sufficient to make par with a decent short game. It was this transformation that led to the advice I've given multiple times in this book: to become less aggressive on the tee and more aggressive around the green. This doesn't mean that you should be lackadaisical with your drive or approach shot, but that with each shot on a hole, your focus and concentration should wax, not wane. Missing a three-foot putt counts the same as driving your ball in a water hazard. Becoming more focused and aggressive as you get closer to the green will improve your score.

This revelation greatly improved my game, but there was a second epiphany about golf that didn't occur to me until later in life. Even with this improved focus around the green and a better approach to each hole, I would often still be frustrated with my score. It turns out that I can't control everything that happens on a golf course, and neither can you. The course difficulty, the conditions, the people you're playing with, and the various travails of life that you bring to the course all impact how well you'll be able to play that day. Understanding that made golf more enjoyable.

I still enjoy hitting the perfect tee shot, and I still enjoy scoring well, but the true enjoyment of golf comes from facing and overcoming the challenges it presents. When you play a new course with a tough slope rating, do you automatically assume that you might as well start drinking now, or do you commit yourself to staying focused and playing your best golf regardless of what the course throws at you? When it's raining or windy, do you assume it will be a miserable day, or do you step up to this challenge with a "British

Open" attitude about the test the weather will provide today? When you can tell in the first few holes that your game has gone south, do you give up, or do you commit to grinding out the best golf you can play in spite of the problems you're experiencing?

Ultimately, the mental game *is* the game of golf. The true test of golf is not how well you can hit the ball or how well you can score, but how well you respond to the various mental challenges that each and every golf round throws at you. You hit a good drive, but it ends up in a divot on the fairway. You hit a good approach, but it takes a hard bounce and runs off the back of the green into the rough. You make a good putt, but the ball lips out. How we respond to these challenges is really what golf is about. Golf can be unfair, and we can't control everything that happens on the course. When stuff happens, accepting the consequences and doing our best to recover is the true challenge of golf. And the greatness of golf is that this is also the true challenge of life.

In a previous chapter, I wrote about setting realistic goals for the round. It is important to set a realistic score for the round based on the course, conditions, and how you've played lately. Even better, set smaller and more attainable goals like the number of holes you score par or less, or the number of holes you limit to no worse than bogey. And if your game is really ugly, you can set a goal for how many solid shots you hit during the round.

Another equally important goal for a round is how you handle the mental challenges. When you four-putted a green, were you able to shake it off and commit to two-putting all the remaining holes? When a wind gust blew your approach shot in the trap, were you able to refocus and get up and down on that hole? When you only needed a bogey on the last hole to break 90 and you hit your tee shot in the woods, did you despair, or did you challenge yourself to make a bogey from there? Responding well to these mental challenges is equally as important as the scoring goals for the round.

Handling transitions is a core theme of this book, and a typical round offers many opportunities to transition: from not playing to playing, from hole to hole, and from shot to shot. The transition following even a good shot can be challenging, especially if you tend to put pressure on yourself after a good shot, but the transition after a bad shot is where you get to test your mental game. The best golfers I know view these transitions as opportunities to test their mental approach. They may get mad initially about the bad shot they just hit, but they quickly shift their focus to the upcoming shot and how best to play the ball as it lies. A bad situation, often of our own doing, becomes a challenge to use our mental skills to transition to doing the best we can under the circumstances.

So about now you're thinking, *My life is hard enough—I play golf to escape life's difficulties.* If you want to escape, go sit on an island beach with a book and a piña colada. If you didn't want a challenge, you wouldn't be playing golf. Unless you play a perfect round of golf, you'll face challenges. And if you are the typical recreational golfer, you'll face lots of challenges. The trick is to make the challenges fun, and that requires embracing these challenges as part of golf, seeing them as opportunities to test your ability to transition from a bad shot to the next shot, and to concentrate on the shot you now face. Successfully facing these challenges is what makes golf the great game that it is.

Chapter 16

Enjoy Golf—an Epilogue

The goal of this book is to provide recreational golfers with specific strategies to improve their mental game and to play the best they can with the current swing they have, however atrocious it may be. Golf is a game of mental transitions: from not playing to playing, from bad hole to next hole, from bad shot to next shot, from inattention to focused attention on the shot at hand. Training yourself to make those transitions and use your mental abilities to manage your game is one of the most challenging and rewarding aspects of the game.

Golf is also a game of assessing risk and reward. Instead of being most aggressive on the tee and most timid around and on the green, most recreational golfers will score better if they are more conservative off the tee and increasingly more aggressive and confident as they get near to and on the green. Remember that the goal of a par four tee shot is simple—to make the hole a reasonable par three on your next shot. And on a par five, the goal of the tee shot is to make the hole an easy par four. Around and on the green, be bold and confident. Less bad outcomes will come from hitting the ball too far than not far enough.

Most importantly, keep the game of golf in perspective. It is not a test of who you are as a person. Nothing important about your life or those you love changes as a result of how well or how badly you play a round of golf. Keep your expectations in check and balance your goals for the round. Are you there more to score well or to enjoy the outdoors and spend time with friends? Golf is a relaxing break from our regular lives, a chance to be outside for hours in places of often striking beauty with people we enjoy being around. Playing well improves the experience, but playing poorly should never rob us of the many joys of golf.

About the Author

Bill Riley, PhD, is a psychologist and recreational golfer who believes golf's mental game strategies can be tailored better to the double-digit handicap duffer. Before retiring in 2022, Dr. Riley served for seventeen years at the National Institutes of Health (NIH), the last seven years as the NIH Associate Director for Behavioral and Social Sciences Research. He received his PhD in clinical psychology from Florida State University and spent most Friday mornings in graduate school sneaking in an early round at the Florida State golf course before going to research meetings. Prior to NIH, he served on the faculty of academic medical schools for fifteen years. He has published over 130 scientific articles and has nearly forty years of professional experience relevant to improving behavioral performance. He is also a long-time recreational golfer who has applied his knowledge of psychology and human behavior to mental game strategies tailored to duffers in *Now That Shot Sucked: Golf's Mental Game for Duffers.*

9 7 9 8 8 8 6 5 4 3 1 5 5